For my parents:
You did a great job raising me—
so I understand your disappointment.

ManWords

MAN CAVE *(noun): a special place in a house (often in the basement) where men can gather and women are discouraged.*

Come on downstairs, guys. I've got the TV in my MAN CAVE set up for the game. And a keg of beer and pretzels.

MANWORDS

REAL WORDS FOR REAL MEN

PONY KEG *(noun): a half-sized beer keg that holds about 62 pints of beer—about enough to last a couple of guys an evening.*

Hey, man, wrestling's on the tube tonight and you've only got a PONY KEG for five of us? You're gonna have to hit a package store in an hour.

PLUS -150- WORDS NO DUDES SHOULD EVER SAY!

JOIST *(noun): typically a long piece of wood supporting either a floor or ceiling. It's important to men mostly because it's typically a long piece of wood.*

I don't have a contractor's license. But I've seen several episodes of This Old House, *so I'm pretty sure I can install a JOIST.*

JEREMY GREENBERG

A adams media

AVON, MASSACHUSETTS

Published by
Adams Media, a division of F+W Media, Inc.
57 Littlefield Street, Avon, MA 02322. U.S.A.
www.adamsmedia.com

ISBN 10: 1-4405-1223-X
ISBN 13: 978-1-4405-1223-0
eISBN 10: 1-4405-1436-4
eISBN 13: 978-1-4405-1436-4

Printed in the United States of America.

10 9 8 7 6 5 4 3 2 1

Library of Congress Cataloging-in-Publication Data
Greenberg, Jeremy.
ManWords / Jeremy Greenberg.
p. cm.
ISBN 978-1-4405-1223-0
1. Men—Humor. I. Title.
PN6231.M45G74 2008
818'.602—dc22
2011010237

This publication is designed to provide accurate and authoritative information with regard to
the subject matter covered. It is sold with the understanding that the publisher is not engaged
in rendering legal, accounting, or other professional advice. If legal advice or other expert
assistance is required, the services of a competent professional person should be sought.
—From a *Declaration of Principles* jointly adopted by a Committee of the American
Bar Association and a Committee of Publishers and Associations

Many of the designations used by manufacturers and sellers to distinguish their product
are claimed as trademarks. Where those designations appear in this book and Adams
Media was aware of a trademark claim, the designations have been printed with initial
capital letters.

Muscles © iStockphoto/MrRoboto
Nose © iStockphot/banderlog

All other interior images © Jupiterimages Corporation

This book is available at quantity discounts for bulk purchases.
For information, please call 1-800-289-0963.

CONTENTS

INTRODUCTION

It's no secret that men have a shared vernacular that only other men understand. You know the words we're talking about; manly words that cause chest hair to spontaneously sprout, power tools to start up with just a glance, and cases of beer to disappear without a trace. Words that let men be . . . well, men. After all, you're a man and if you want to have a bromance with your wingman, tap out of a board meeting, or walk off an injury so painful that it knocks the wind right out of you, you need to know how to express yourself. And here, in this celebration of all things manly, you'll find every ManWord ever uttered.

However, as you probably already know, some words are just more masculine than others. To help you know which words will only inspire a fist bump, and which words are worthy of a ticker-tape parade, we've rated each word based on its manliness. After all, we want you to be all the man you can be.

So, whether you're a working stiff, a single guy tossing back shooters on a weeknight, or a married man who bravely faces the weekends with a weed whacker in one hand and an oversized set of grilling utensils in the other, here you'll find the words you need to know to keep your testosterone pumping. Enjoy!

Chapter 1

I'M NOT *HURT*, I'M *PISSED*!

**(words that mask emotion—
which is the feeling a guy gets in his stomach
telling him it's time to start drinking)**

Throughout history men have been notoriously incapable of expressing their feelings. Don't feel bad if this is you. In today's society, we're encouraged to be sensitive and wear our emotions on our sleeves. Fortunately, there's an antidote: this chapter on masking emotions. You'll love it—but don't admit it, or your friends will call you a sissy.

ANTISOCIAL *(adjective)*

what women will call a guy who doesn't want to go with her to some lame-ass party.

> The women from my knitting group are lots of fun! I think the reason you won't go to their party is that you're just ANTISOCIAL.

> *I was lousy in school. Real screwed up. A moron. I was*
> ***ANTISOCIAL** and didn't bother with the other kids. A really*
> *bad student. I didn't have any brains. I didn't know what I*
> *was doing there. That's why I became an actor.*
> ANTHONY HOPKINS

 **APESHIT** *(adverb)*

as opposed to losing one's shit, which is more of an implosion, going *apeshit* is to lose one's f'ing mind in a more exterior fashion.

> If the store tries to give me store credit for my return I'm going to go APESHIT on the cashier and knock over that display of cheap cologne.

ASS CLOWN *(noun)*

there are chefs and top chefs, and there are clowns and *ass clowns*—a grand distinction only earned by a handful of idiots.

> The class clown grew up to be nothing more than an ASS CLOWN.

ASSHOLE *(noun)*

typically a guy who makes more money, has a hotter wife, or is simply better than other men at stuff. Unlike a douche bag, an *asshole* can still be respectable.

> That ASSHOLE has won three Super Bowls, and two supermodels.

> *That's the miracle of babies, their ability to lay bare the*
> *tender, beating hearts of raging **ASSHOLES**.*
> HEATHER ARMSTRONG (AKA DOOCE), AMERICAN BLOGGER

ASSWIPE *(noun)*
an asshole's sidekick; someone who cleans up the messes an asshole makes.
That ASSWIPE had better stick with his friends, or he'll get torn apart.

AWESOME *(adjective)*
so great that it inspires awe; best used when describing hamburgers and tits.
If you knock on a watermelon and it sounds hollow, you know it'll be AWESOME.

BAD *(adjective)*
good; best used preceding "motherfucker."
Oedipus Rex was one BAD motherfucker.

BADASS *(noun)*
an alpha male. It's one of the few terms guys can use to express admiration for another man without sounding like they've got a man crush.
That guy who can burp the "Star-Spangled Banner" is a total BADASS.

> *Hey Ripley, don't worry. Me and my squad of ultimate*
> ***BADASSES** will protect you.*
>
> ALIENS

BADMOUTH *(verb)*
to speak ill of someone or something; it's like talking shit, but a bit more formal.
The fact that my Match.com date looked nothing like her photo left me no choice but to BADMOUTH her all over my Facebook page.

BAG OF SHIT *(noun)*
a bag containing shit, or a guy who reminds you of a bag containing shit. A good substitute if you've already used "asshole" too much that day.

My history professor's a complete BAG OF SHIT. He keeps insisting that Pol Pot is not a type of marijuana.

BALLSY *(adjective)*
tough, not afraid of taking risks or being hurt—pretty much the opposite of actual balls.

He was known as a very BALLSY juggler.

BASTARD *(noun)*
a child born out of wedlock; what a woman calls a man who leaves town after impregnating her out of wedlock.

I can't believe that BASTARD wouldn't take a DNA test.

> *Every now and then when your life gets complicated and the weasels start closing in, the only cure is to load up on heinous chemicals and then drive like a **BASTARD** from Hollywood to Las Vegas . . . with the music at top volume and at least a pint of ether.*
> HUNTER S. THOMPSON

BELLICOSE *(adjective)*
hostile, wanting war; imagine if a Klingon and a strung-out supermodel had offspring.

Lance became BELLICOSE when the drugstore cashier said they were out of cortisone cream.

MANWORDS

BERSERK *(adverb)*
violently apeshit; from an ancient Scandinavian legend about the first guy to watch a soccer match.

All I did was tell Sven that his fish sandwich stank to high hell, and the guy went BERSERK.

BITCHSLAP *(noun, verb)*
a slap to the face with an open palm; a verbal assault to which there is no defense.

When Michael forgot to pick up the beer for the party, I was so upset I BITCHSLAPPED him.

Someday, you're gonna get BITCHSLAPPED and I'm not gonna do a thing to stop it.
10 THINGS I HATE ABOUT YOU

BITCHY *(adjective)*
a term best used when a guy wants his friend to do what he wants. Implying that a guy's being bitchy has with it the powerful implication that he's not even complaining like a man.

You said you'd help me move. So stop being so BITCHY and let me tie a refrigerator to the roof of your Ford Escort.

BONEHEAD *(noun)*
not as dumb as a dumbass, but more stupid than a shit-for-brains, because at least the latter has brains—even if they're shit.

When Frankenstein drove off with his coffee on the roof of his car, the other monsters called him a BONEHEAD.

DUDE, DON'T SAY IT: BEAUTY MARK

What It Means: what a woman will call a facial mole or some other hideous deformity.
It's Only Okay When: you politely explain to your girlfriend what they now have laser-removal treatments for.

BRAWL *(noun, verb)*
a noisy fight; imagine if two cats were having sex, but were also drunk and not cats, but rednecks.
Two chicks started to BRAWL when they both showed up wearing the same outfit.

BROMANCE *(noun)*
a close friendship between two heterosexual guys which, even though they talk on the phone all the time, and go clothes shopping together, doesn't make them gay.
Peter was involved in a very serious BROMANCE with a guy in his fantasy league.

BROTHER FROM ANOTHER MOTHER *(noun)*
a friend who is so close that the only thing you don't have in common is the bloodline from whence you came.
How could you sleep with my mom? I thought you were my BROTHER FROM ANOTHER MOTHER? Now you might become my stepfather from another mother.

 BROWN-NOSE *(verb)*
to treat another human being better than they deserve for purposes of survival or gain.
My golden retriever BROWN-NOSES me all the time.

MANWORDS

CALLOUS *(adjective)*
a desired quality in both a man's feet, and his attitude toward anything deli-cate and beautiful. Originally the word just referred to having big pads of unfeeling, dead skin. But over time, women realized this is also a pretty good word to describe most men.

> **My feet are all calloused, but I'm so CALLOUS that I don't give a damn.**

DUDE, DON'T SAY IT: BERET

What It Means: a hat fancied by Frenchmen and artists.
It's Only Okay When: discussing the military elite forces called the Green Berets. When a guy's that badass he almost needs to wear a beret out of fairness to guys who aren't.

CANDY ASS *(noun)*
a person who is afraid and cowardly because he believes himself to be as delicate as candy; the only honest fear for a candy ass is a trail of ants.

> **The gingerbread man who refused to stand up for himself was a total CANDY ASS.**

CHICKENSHIT *(adjective)*
second only to fraidy-cat in utter cowardliness; best used when trying to goad someone into doing something stupid.

> **Come on, why won't you jump off the roof of that eight-story build-ing? What are you, CHICKENSHIT?**

CHILLAX *(verb)*
a combination of "chill" and "relax"; best used to appear cool while telling someone else to mellow out.

> **Dude, CHILLAX! I'll stall the cops.**

DUDE, DON'T SAY IT: COUTURE

What It Means: really expensive, custom-made clothing.
It's Only Okay When: trying to describe the $30 airbrushed T-shirt that you got at the flea market.

COCKSUCKER *(noun)*
a general insult; rivals "douche bag" as one of the worst things a man can be called.
> Next time I see the guy who told my mom I was smoking weed I'm going to kill that COCKSUCKER.

COOL *(adjective)*
the ability to appear not to give a shit.
> When the hostess told Steve and his date that there was a thirty-minute wait for a table, he played it COOL and slipped her a twenty, which promptly got him the best seat in the Olive Garden.

CRAPPY *(adjective)*
not quite shitty, but substandard.
> The drunken girl at the barbeque begged me for sex. At first things were going pretty well, but the night turned CRAPPY when she vomited and passed out.

 **CROCK OF SHIT** *(noun)*
an untruth; what liars bring to picnics.
> He said he used Tabasco in this stew, but that's a CROCK OF SHIT.

DAD *(noun)*

the person whose life you ruined by being born; the guy who gave you your first beer; the asshole who made you mow the lawn; the person you'll become when you have kids.

My DAD told me he didn't start drinking until I was born.

DAMN *(interjection)*

what a man says when he experiences moderate disappointment—like when McDonald's stopped supersizing food.

DAMN. Someone stole my girlfriend's panties off of the clothesline in the back yard.

DANG *(interjection)*

"damn" for wimps; best used when a guy's trying to appear reformed at his parole hearing.

When I get out of prison, I'm going to kill my DANG lawyer.

DUDE, DON'T SAY IT: DECOR

What It Means: doesn't matter, no dude should use a word with an accented vowel—it is the extended pinkie finger of punctuation.
It's Only Okay When: explaining to your date that your unmade bed is actually a very hip form of décor called the "natural look."

DICKHEAD *(noun)*

a jerk.

That guy who is into collecting Richard Nixon memorabilia is a total DICKHEAD.

DICKWAD *(noun)*

not smart enough to be a dickhead (as it would imply that he had a head), but not as wild and crazy as a dickweed.

That DICKWAD went to jail for soliciting prostitution—from a woman in a police uniform.

DICKWEED *(noun)*
while most dicks are people who have been made unpleasant through bad parenting, or a lack of love, dickweeds can grow unpleasant in any environment, very quickly, and often require chemicals to keep them under control.

That gardener who planted the dandelions is a total DICKWEED.

DING-A-LING *(noun)*
an idiot who doesn't quite merit being called a dumbshit or shit-for-brains; best used for calling a waiter or waitress an idiot while on a first date, so the woman thinks you're sensitive.

I can't believe the silly DING-A-LING forgot our drink order.

DINGBAT *(noun)*
stupid, but kind of in a cute way; best used to describe a really beautiful woman who forgets to wear underwear.

That girl in the bikini we met at the car show was a total DINGBAT.

DUDE, DON'T SAY IT: DECORATIVE

What It Means: not functional, purely to look at and not for touching, and therefore useless.
It's Only Okay When: you explain that you didn't know when your mother-in-law finds teeth marks in her plastic fruit.

DIPSHIT *(noun)*
another term for idiot; best used for people who chew tobacco, or are too stupid to slow down for dips in the road.

That DIPSHIT tried to tell me he makes his own ice cream.

DON'T FUCK WITH ME *(phrase)*
a warning men will emit when they are reaching the threshold of tolerable annoyances; best used right before inquiring if someone would like to get his ass kicked.

DON'T FUCK WITH ME unless your health care covers hospital visits!

DON'T FUCK WITH ME fellas. This ain't my first time at the rodeo.
MOMMY DEAREST

DOOFUS *(noun)*
a clueless idiot; it's key for men to know that, unlike a dumbass, dipshit, or dumbfuck, there are no circumstances in which a guy can meet girls with a doofus in his crew. But, the doofus friend is good for playing or watching sports, drinking (a time in which he somehow becomes less of a doofus), or helping you move.

Did you have to bring Johnny? I know he's your cousin, but the guy's a DOOFUS.

DORKWAD *(noun)*
a guy who is dorky to the point of doing things like wearing fanny packs in public, opening conversations by discussing a love of hard-boiled eggs, and in extreme cases, having a tattoo of his *Second Life* avatar.

That DORKWAD just told me my car's not parked within eighteen inches of the curb.

DOUCHE BAG *(noun)*

a guy who exhibits moral qualities and pleasantness similar to that of a popular feminine hygiene product.

That guy's a total DOUCHE BAG. I'd never cheat on a girl that hot.

DUMBASS *(noun)*

someone of equal or lesser intelligence than a buttocks; best used when describing someone as harmlessly stupid, as opposed to a dumbfuck or a shit for brains, whose stupidity can be troublesome.

That donkey who forgot the trail to the bottom of the Grand Canyon is a real DUMBASS.

DUMBFUCK *(noun, adjective)*

a degree more stupid than a dumbass, and one less than a doofus. "Dumbfuck" should be reserved for profound acts of stupidity.

I can't believe that DUMBFUCK thought the stripper would actually hook up with him in the champagne room.

DUDE, DON'T SAY IT: DENOUEMENT

What It Means: if a man knows this word, it means he's seen way too much theater. The only good part is that "denouement" actually means "the ending" or "the best part" of a story. And most men would agree that whatever they're being forced to watch, for them the ending will be the best part.

It's Only Okay When: loudly asking a wife or girlfriend, "Is this the denouement?" five minutes after the play has started.

DUMBSHIT *(noun)*

an idiot whose parents were a bunch of dumbasses, and consequently produced a real dumbshit.

That DUMBSHIT fell asleep with a cigarette on his chest and now has third-degree burns.

DWEEB *(noun)*
the only person capable of being a bigger dorkwad than a dorkwad. Both dork and dweeb start at the same nerd genus, but whereas a dorkwad might be smart, a dweeb is also awkward and stupid.
That guy who always writes in his own electoral candidates is a total DWEEB.

FLYING FUCK *(phrase)*
what men should never give.
So you won your fantasy league. You know what? I don't give a FLYING FUCK.

FUCKFACE *(noun)*
less of an idiot than a fuckhead, this person's level of fuck is limited to just the face.
That FUCKFACE puked in my sister's car.

FUCKHEAD *(noun)*
an irksome person of poor breeding; best used when referring to a good friend who did something stupid; for less well-known idiots, use the more formal put-downs from the "ass" (dumbass) or "shit" (dumbshit) class of insults.
That FUCKHEAD puked in my backpack.

FUCKING A *(interjection)*
can mean "really," "are you kidding," or "that sucks, I'm angry"; and can also be used by a man with an alphabet fetish to describe what he dreamt he was doing last night.
FUCKING A, man! I can't believe you forgot the tickets!

GALOOT *(noun)*
a clumsy fool; best used by big-eared cartoon rabbits with a knack for out-smarting hunters, as well as men who like to get high and talk about cartoons.
That big-eared GALOOT keeps putting TNT in my piano.

GAME *(adjective)*
a way of describing any skill used to make money, excel in sports, get laid, dominate at video games, or basically do well at anything else in life. "Game" has the magical ability of making anything a guy's talking about sound superficial, and is therefore very valuable when it comes to diminishing the appearance that he might actually give a shit about something.

When it comes to playing Dungeons and Dragons, I have mad GAME.

> *He got* **GAME.**
> MICHAEL JORDAN

GIVE A SHIT *(phrase)*
to care about.

My girlfriend was pissed when I didn't complete the chores on the honeydo list, but you know what? I don't GIVE A SHIT.

> *Rehabilitated? It's just a bullshit word. So you go on and stamp your form, sonny, and stop wasting my time. Because to tell you the truth, I don't* **GIVE A SHIT.**
> THE SHAWSHANK REDEMPTION

GIVING YOU SHIT *(phrase)*
to tease, usually playfully and in good spirit; men should remember it's good etiquette that when being given shit, always give shit right back.

The sewage truck didn't really empty its contents into your swimming pool. I was just GIVING YOU SHIT.

GLAD HAND *(noun)*
an insincere and fakely enthusiastic greeting; such as when meeting an ex-girlfriend's new boyfriend.
> **I knew right away that my GLAD HAND wasn't appreciated by my fiance's dad when I met him for the first time.**

GNARLY *(adjective)*
means both "incredibly gross" and "incredibly awesome."
> **Wathcing my wife give birth was totally GNARLY.**

GOING POSTAL *(phrase)*
to go crazy; taken from the tendency of postal workers to flip out and gun down a bunch of people; best used to describe a guy who has accepted shit his entire life and finally decided he's not going to take it any more.
> **When the package didn't arrive, I got in my car with plans of GOING POSTAL.**

GO PISS UP A ROPE *(phrase)*
a polite request to be left alone.
> **When my mom woke me up at 9:30 on a Saturday morning I told her to GO PISS UP A ROPE. So what if I live in her basement!**

GUTS *(noun)*
courage; best used when needing to describe a brave woman who doesn't have "balls."
> **It takes a lot of GUTS to enter a hotdog-eating contest.**

HAIRY EYEBALL *(noun)*
a very angry or judgmental glare; best used when the jerk staring has a ridiculous goatee.
> **All I did was take his parking spot, and that asshole gave me the HAIRY EYEBALL.**

HANG OUT *(verb)*

The only permissible way to describe how men spend time together.

Men should be advised that while HANGING OUT, nothing should ever actually HANG OUT.

> ## DUDE, DON'T SAY IT: HEMLINE
>
> **What It Means:** the bottom edge of a dress or skirt; all a guy needs to notice is if a skirt is short—other than that, the woman might as well be wearing pants.
> **It's Only Okay When:** explaining what you don't like about Mennonite fashion.

HARDBALL *(noun)*

being uncompromisingly tough; most often used by men who are buying used shit off of Craigslist.

I don't mean to play HARDBALL, but I will offer you $30 for the sewing table and not a penny more!

HARDCORE *(adjective)*

"hardcore" is a term to help describe anything taken to the extreme. Hardcore skateboarders do moves most people would never try, as do hardcore porn stars.

Just because I'm a HARDCORE Nickelback fan doesn't mean I'm tone-deaf.

HEAD UP HIS/HER ASS *(phrase)*

completely clueless; men are advised that it's better to have one's head up one's ass than to be a dumbshit, because one can always remove one's head from one's ass.

You're not gonna learn shit with your HEAD UP YOUR ASS! Or are you?

DUDE, DON'T SAY IT: FRAGRANT

What It Means: when shit smells nice. The proper term is, "This shit smells nice!"
It's Only Okay When: trying to hide the fact that instead of doing laundry, you just covered your clothes in Lysol.

HELLACIOUS *(adjective)*
so awful it's like being in hell; best used to describe most visits to in-laws.
Watching *My Big Fat Greek Wedding* was the most HELLACIOUS two hours of my entire life.

HONEST *(adverb)*
means "bullshit"; best used when one wants to hide the fact that something's bullshit.
I didn't flood the engine, HONEST.

HOSTILE *(adjective)*
antagonistic; men are advised not to waste hostility on bigger people who can kick their asses, but instead to save their hostility and take it out on people through meaningless conversations about sports, or about Pamela Anderson's chest size.
I don't know why he's accusing me of being HOSTILE. All I said was that anyone who wears skinny jeans deserves to have his ass kicked.

I KNOW HOW YOU FEEL *(phrase)*
what a man says when he doesn't know how someone feels, and isn't interested in discussing it.
No man, totally . . . that blind date must have been tough, I KNOW HOW YOU FEEL.

I'M NOT HURT, I'M PISSED!

I WOULDN'T FUCK HER WITH HIS DICK *(phrase)* 💪💪💪💪💪💪
how a man politely mentions a lack of sexual attraction.

I don't care if I was completely drunk, and no one would ever find out, I WOULDN'T FUCK HER WITH HIS DICK.

DUDE, DON'T SAY IT: I'M LATE

What It Means: how a woman tells a guy she might be pregnant.
It's Only Okay When: a man must repeat the woman's "I'm late" just to clarify, and because he's so happy, he's practically in tears.

ICE MAN/MAVERICK/GOOSE (Top Gun *nicknames*) *(noun)* 💪💪💪💪
whenever one guy needs to mock another, one of the most effective ways is to call him one of the nicknames made famous in the Tom Cruise homoerotic thriller *Top Gun.*

You think you're real manly in that jumpsuit, don't ya MAVERICK.

JACKASS *(noun)* 💪
a stupid person; a wildly successful TV show about watching stupid people risk their lives; the least offensive term in the "ass" family of insults.

Since everyone else is a dumbass, the promotion went to David, who is just a JACKASS.

JERK OFF, JERK-OFF *(verb, noun)*
to masturbate; a person who is an annoying time waster. Jerk-offs are not as malicious as douche bags, but are bigger assholes than guys who are dicks.

When Pete JERKED OFF in the shower before his big date, he felt like a huge JERK-OFF.

JIVE-ASS TURKEY *(noun)*
a sucka fool who thinks he all that, but in truth he ain't shit.

Ain't no way I'm inviting that JIVE-ASS TURKEY to Thanksgiving.

KISS ASS *(noun)*

someone who uses the very unmanly tactics of compliments, flattery, and favors to get something they want; the only difference between a kiss ass and brown-nose is location, location, location.

That sportscaster who practically swooned over his team's quarterback in order to obtain an interview was a real KISS ASS.

KISS MY ASS *(phrase)*

when a man wishes someone would go away, or stop pestering him, the annoyed guy will invite the pest to kiss his ass, to which almost all men politely decline.

That dog-whisperer guy can KISS MY ASS.

KNUCKLEHEAD *(noun)*

slightly smarter than a bonehead, since knuckles have moving parts, but definitely dumber than a numbskull.

The KNUCKLEHEAD was fingered in the ring heist when he gave the finger to the jeweler's wife.

KVETCH *(verb, noun)*

an important word if a man ever decides to date a Jewish chick. It means to complain to the point of making a man want to rip his own penis off—which is actually where Jews got the tradition of circumcision.

She's cute, but she KVETCHED so much I kissed her just to shut her up.

LOSE MY/YOUR/HIS SHIT *(phrase)*

to go crazy. The term originates from medieval times, when people were so poor that all they had was shit. And if a poor serf should lose his shit, he'd be so upset that he'd really lose his shit.

If the elevator doesn't arrive soon I'm going to LOSE MY SHIT.

LOSER *(noun)*
person with no ambition, job, or prospects; someone who always loses at life.

Dude, you bought that woman drinks all night and you didn't even get her number? You are such a LOSER.

> Mac: Wow, so that's the saddest thing I've ever heard. You guys are **LOSERS**.
>
> Dennis: How are we **LOSERS**, dude?
>
> Mac: Well, maybe it boils down to this, smart guy: computers are for **LOSERS**.
>
> Dennis: And you're drinking a beer at 8 o'clock in the morning.
>
> Mac: Whatever, dude, irrelevant.
>
> IT'S ALWAYS SUNNY IN PHILADELPHIA

LUNKHEAD *(noun)*
idiot.

Last night I cruised by Wendy's to see if that LUNKHEAD who works the Fryolator would give me some free chicken—if you know what I mean.

MAMA'S BOY *(noun)*
a boy who loves his mother more than his own self-respect.

She knew the relationship was over when that MAMA'S BOY screamed, "Read me a bedtime story!" while they were making love.

> I've dated the sweetest **MAMA'S BOY**, the musician rocker, the struggling artist—basically a lot of people without jobs.
>
> ALYSSA MILANO

MAN CRUSH *(noun)*
when a man has a non-gay infatuation with another man. Signs of a man crush include excessive talking about the other man, or asking your wife to call out his name during sex.

I don't have a MAN CRUSH on my brother-in-law! I just think he's really cool to hang out with.

MAN HUG *(noun)*
just as there's the five-second rule, in which any piece of food left on the ground for less than five seconds is magically still clean, so too is there a rule that any hug between two men lasting less than three seconds keeps them from becoming gay.

Nobody at poker night was willing to tell Bill that his MAN HUGS bordered on frontal dong clanks.

MARY *(noun)*
old-timey slang for a "good girl"; mostly used to insult a guy for being a goody two-shoes.

Come on, MARY. We all paid the $500 buy-in for the Texas Hold-Em tournament. Now it's your turn.

MEATHEAD *(noun)*
an idiot; derived from the idea that a man's head is full of meat rather than full of brains.

Not only did she accuse her boyfriend of thinking with his dick, she added insult to injury and said that he was a complete MEATHEAD.

MOSH *(noun)*
the only kind of dancing where there aren't any women, but a dude doesn't feel gay; also known as slam dancing, or not being hugged enough as a child.

At the Metallica concert, I got cock-punched in the MOSH pit.

MOTHERFUCKER (*noun*)
this word's meaning is dependent on the tone with which it's said. It can be a term of respect, or derision, depending on what the speaker thinks about the motherfucker he's talking about.

I just knew that MOTHERFUCKER would be made sole beneficiary in his mom's will.

> *Low blows? Low blows? Huh! **MOTHERFUCKER** you're fittin' to die!*
>
> MIKE TYSON

MOUTH BREATHER (*noun*)
a person who is so stupid that he's yet to figure out he can shut his mouth and breathe through his nose; characterized by staring slack-jawed at the beef jerky aisle of 7-Eleven.

My wingman couldn't figure out why no one wanted to date his brother. Sure he was a nice guy, but he was also an overalls-wearing MOUTH BREATHER with a trucker's tan.

NAPOLEONIC COMPLEX (*noun*)
describes an effective strategy for short people to appear taller by acting like assholes; it's a scientific fact that the same part of the brain that thinks someone's short also decides if he's an asshole—and it can't do both simultaneously.

My boss didn't have a NAPOLEONIC COMPLEX until he got a job in the NBA.

NO PAIN NO GAIN (*phrase*)
pain with no gain is fine for characters in foreign films. But real men gotta get something from their suffering, like bigger biceps, or an injury that qualifies them for workers' compensation.

I just pulled my Achille's tendon when I moved the wrong way playing Wii. But you know what they say, NO PAIN NO GAIN.

DUDE, DON'T SAY IT: NEST

What It Means: the way a pregnant woman rearranges the house (read "throws out all your favorite stuff") in preparation for the baby. If you know this term, it means a woman is actively trying to replace that part of your brain that stores your fantasy football stats with instructions for how to change a diaper.

It's Only Okay When: your favorite football team's mascot is an Eagle or Hawk, and their stadium is referred to as a nest.

NO SHIT *(phrase)*

means, "Really, you don't say"; best used when a guy is about to accept something as fact.

You're telling me the male seahorse is the one who gives birth? NO SHIT.

NUMBNUTS *(noun)*

more of an instinctive idiot than a numbskull, equivalent to a dumbass, and slightly better off than a shit for brains—because nuts can thaw, but shit is shit.

Hey NUMBNUTS, no one cares how cold you are. You don't turn the heat up in the ice-fishing tent!

NUMBSKULL *(noun)*

the least offensive in the "numb" class of insults; best used when someone isn't quite a dumbass, and doesn't deserve to be called a stupid fuck.

That NUMBSKULL refuses to wear a helmet when he takes his rice burner out on the highway.

OFF THE HOOK *(phrase)*

something that is excellent or awesome; best used by a fifty-year-old man in a desperate attempt to connect with his teenage son.

Hey son, your FaceSpace account is OFF THE HOOK.

OPEN A CAN OF WHOOP ASS *(phrase)*
to kick a guy's ass with such incredible power, it's as though the ass kicker was fortified with something one could find in a can—like beer.

> **I'm going to OPEN A CAN OF WHOOP ASS on my paperboy if he keeps getting the Sunday edition stuck on the roof.**

PAIN IS WEAKNESS LEAVING THE BODY *(phrase)*
perhaps the most effective phrase ever invented to trick men into suffering. However, it is a good, positive mantra if you ever find yourself in a lot of pain.

> **Don't worry about all the blood gushing out of your head wound, that just a bunch of WEAKNESS LEAVING THE BODY.**

DUDE, DON'T SAY IT: POTPOURRI

What It Means: a small bowl of dried flowers that women put in bathrooms to mask . . . other smells.
It's Only Okay When: looking for a good place to put out a cigarette.

PANSY *(noun)*
unlike a pussy, who can be capable yet afraid, a pansy is a delicate wimp—the kind of guy who can sprain his wrist when giving a high-five.

> **That PANSY won't eat rocky road ice cream, for fear of chipping a tooth.**

PECKERHEAD *(noun)*
an idiot who specializes in making a mess of situations every time he opens his mouth.

> **That PECKERHEAD is always spouting nonsense.**

PECKERWOOD *(noun)*
a derogatory term for a redneck.

> **My neighbor is such a PECKERWOOD that he woke me up at 5 A.M. on a Saturday by shooting BB rounds at my bird feeder.**

PENCIL NECK *(noun)*
a scrawny person with a red rubbery ass.
   That PENCIL NECK left little pieces of crap all over my paper.

PEON *(noun)*
a person of such low social status that a man would pee on him for the sake of keeping the ground dry.
   Despite standing for long hours, the PEON never had athlete's foot.

 PISS ANT *(noun)*
someone of little worth or importance; best used by drill sergeants to describe a ragtag bunch of recruits that somehow manage to make it through basic training.
   Tell those PISS ANTS that this ain't no picnic!

PISS OFF *(verb)*
to make angry.
   Don't PISS OFF your girlfriend around the holidays—unless you *want* to spend New Year's Eve sitting on your couch, eating Chinese food alone.

> Can you **PISS OFF** a Puerto Rican and live to tell about it?
> JENNIFER LOPEZ

PISSED OFF *(adjective)*
irritated, angry.
   When the new blade on John's compound miter saw broke he was so PISSED OFF that he hired a contractor to do the job instead.

> The good news is that Jesus is coming back. The bad news is that he's really **PISSED OFF**.
> BOB HOPE

I'M NOT *HURT*, I'M *PISSED*!

PLAYER-HATER (*noun*)
most commonly refers to anyone trying to interfere with a guy's ability to have financial or sexual success. Men like the term "player-hater" because it's a way to say someone's jealous without sounding bitchy.
I can't believe it. Right as that hottie was about to come up to me to get my digits, some PLAYER-HATER walked up and asked if I still live with my mom.

PRETTY BOY (*noun*)
a guy whose attractiveness borders on the feminine, and therefore annoys men who are either jealous, or confused.
That PRETTY BOY's sister is actually really hot.

PUNK-ASS (*noun*)
a man who lacks both courage and morals, and probably owes a few people money. Also, a guy who just does lame, annoying stuff.
That PUNK-ASS snuck onto my farm, and spray-painted "Black Flag rules" onto my donkey.

PUSSY (*noun*)
a wimp; the female sex organ. Ironically, an actual pussy is quite strong if one considers what it endures during childbirth. Nonetheless, no guy wants to be called a pussy.
That PUSSY spends one week a month finding homes for orphans.

RAGE (*noun*)
violent anger; one of the few acceptable male emotions; best experienced while driving.
The drunken airline pilot flew off in a RAGE.

RAUNCHY (*adjective*)
crude and vulgar; the condition of the average male conversation.
I can't believe she thought that describing my penis as a baby bazooka was RAUNCHY.

RIGHTEOUS *(adjective)*
totally good and awesome; best used to describe seemingly insignificant things that provide a disproportionate amount of joy.
That was an f'ing RIGHTEOUS steak taco!

SARCASM *(noun)*
one of the few appropriate ways in which a man may be critical, other than by saying that something is bullshit or sucks; characterized by being mockingly ironic.
I'm married today because, on our first date, I told my wife her hair looked nice but she failed to get my SARCASM.

 **SICK** *(aka sick-ass) (adjective)*
totally fucking awesome; frequently used by surfers, skateboarders, and hypochondriacs.
That guy with the runny nose was a SICK kazoo player.

SMART ASS *(noun)*
someone who enjoys embarrassing others through a demonstration of his knowledge; a know-it-all. Men are advised that it's the most fun to be a smart ass toward an authority figure who happens to be a dumbass.
The donkey who could count with his hoof was a real SMART ASS.

SMOOTH MOVE EX-LAX *(phrase)*
How one guy sarcastically lets another guy know that he just messed up.
SMOOTH MOVE EX-LAX, you painted the ambulance wrong and people are going to think that they'll have to get out of the way because an ecnalubma is approaching them.

SON OF A BITCH *(interjection, noun)*
means, "Gosh darnit, that sure isn't swell." Also is a person who is a jerk because his mom didn't hug him enough.
> I can't believe that SON OF A BITCH has been texting my booty call behind my back.

STRAIGHT-UP *(adverb)*
means, "No bullshit. I'm serious"; it is obvious men would see something that describes their erect penises ("straight" and "up") as being a representation of purity and truth.
> I told her STRAIGHT-UP that there was a chance I might've lied about my age when we first met.

DUDE, DON'T SAY IT: SPARKLING WINE

What It Means: basically, it's Champagne without the fancy name.
It's Only Okay When: no real booze is available.

STRUT HIS/HER/YOUR STUFF *(phrase)*
to show off.
> The senior citizen really decided to STRUT HIS STUFF during the meat raffle at the VFW.

SUCK *(verb)*
to really stink at something.
> So we're in the parking lot, but our tickets are sitting on your kitchen counter? Man, you SUCK!

> *What's the difference between a Democrat and a Republican? A Democrat blows, a Republican SUCKS!*
> LEWIS BLACK

SUCKS TO BE YOU *(phrase)*
How one man comforts another man following a disappointment.
> Wow, you got all of your teeth knocked out by a flying hockey puck and can only eat through a straw? SUCKS TO BE YOU!

SUMBITCH *(noun)*
slang for son of a bitch, very popular with southerners.
> That SUMBITCH can't marry my cousin until I break up with her first!

 TALK SHIT *(verb)*
to say something nasty, usually for purposes of starting a fight.
> I was in the men's room taking care of business when I heard my friend TALK SHIT about me to my boss.

TAP OUT *(verb)*
a term from UFC (Ultimate Fighting Championship) that refers to a fighter slamming his hand on the mat to signal to the ref that his ass has officially been kicked. Also used by guys whenever they need to communicate that something in life has officially kicked their asses. By using a UFC term, the guy can avoid seeming like a pussy.
> The line to get into this bar sucks. I'm TAPPIN' OUT and going home.

THE SHIT *(noun)*
a great person; best used when there's a bit of jealousy or resentment. Although the guy being talked about might be "the shit," secretly one wishes he was *just* shit.
> That successful plumber is THE SHIT.

DUDE, DON'T SAY IT: THE NEW BLACK

What It Means: the color or thing that is this year's hottest fashion. The proper term is, "People are going totally apeshit for . . ."
It's Only Okay When: bubonic plague should somehow re-emerge.

UNCOOL (adjective)　　　　　　

not nice; best used when the person pointing out the not-niceness wants to make sure he still appears cool.

Dude, telling that girl you weren't married and that your kids were nephews was very UNCOOL.

> *The only true currency in this bankrupt world is what you share with someone else when you're UNCOOL.*
> ALMOST FAMOUS

WALK IT OFF (phrase)　　　　　

a means by which a man can heal serious injuries and ailments by walking in a semicircle while grimacing in pain.

Dude, it looks like you tore your Achilles tendon. Just WALK IT OFF, bro.

WANKER (noun)　　　　　　

a masturbating idiot.

That WANKER had no idea his webcam was on.

WEIRDO *(noun)*
an eccentric, deranged person; characterized by fearlessly wearing fanny packs, proudly owning a calculator watch, and always saying "later gator" at every departure.

That WEIRDO said that he always carries $20 worth of quarters just in case aliens wipe out our cell phones, and he has to use a land line.

WHAT CRAWLED UP YOUR/HIS ASS AND DIED *(phrase)*
a way of asking why someone's in a bad mood; this of course assumes the person is from a culture in which dead anal parasites are a cause for discomfort.

Did your girlfriend dump you? Did you rear-end someone on your way in to work today? No? Then WHAT CRAWLED UP YOUR ASS AND DIED?

WHAT THE HELL *(phrase)*
How a man says, "Why not?"

She asked me if I was ready to meet her parents, and I was like, "Sure. WHAT THE HELL?"

DUDE, DON'T SAY IT: WRAPPING PAPER

What It Means: decorative printed paper that women wrap presents in when they could just as easily leave it in the bag, or cover it in newspaper.
It's Only Okay When: explaining to your wife what you will never, ever, ever save after opening a gift.

WHATEVER, DUDE *(phrase)*
what one man says to politely ignore the moronic comments of another.

I was like, WHATEVER, DUDE. Even if you are great at *Centipede*, I'm not giving you a free quarter when your game's over.

WHERE THE RUBBER MEETS THE ROAD *(phrase)*
the bottom line.

A lot of guys say they always use condoms, but all of the surprise pregnancies that occur suggest that something different happens WHERE THE RUBBER MEETS THE ROAD.

> *There are smart ways to solve some of our problems so there's more money on the ground* **WHERE THE RUBBER MEETS THE ROAD.**
> STEVE WESTLY

WHO DIED AND MADE YOU BOSS *(phrase)*
means "What makes you think that you're in charge"; this is a common phrase meant to challenge authority, to which the proper response is, "Don't no one have to die to make me know I can whoop your ass."

She was like, WHO DIED AND MADE YOU BOSS, and I was like, my dad—his succession plan was in his will.

WINDBAG *(noun)*
a man or woman who won't shut up.

That WINDBAG can blow me if he thinks I want to hear any more of his stupid ideas about renewable sources of energy.

YO BITCH! *(interjection)*
a formal summons of either a female, or a male of lower rank; also frequently used by females as an antecedent to, "You betta stay away from my man, ho!"

YO BITCH! I think you're gonna win it all at this year's Westminster dog show.

YOUNIVERSE *(noun)*

the narcissistic belief (usually held by recent college grads and gen-Xers) that the universe revolves around them.

Pete's YOUNIVERSE came crashing down when he lost his job and spent the next three months sleeping in his parents' basement.

YOUR ASS IS GRASS AND I'M THE LAWN MOWER *(phrase)*

on the surface, threatening to mow someone's ass may not seem like the most masculine of threats. But it is great quick little intimidation line if one is about to fight, or give a woman a Brazilian.

So, I looked the Chia Pet right in the eyes and said, "YOUR ASS IS GRASS, AND I'M THE LAWN MOWER."

YOUR MAMA *(phrase)*

the answer to any question that a guy doesn't want to answer.

He asked, "Where did you get that Eskimo Pie?" and I said, "YOUR MAMA, that's where."

DUDE, DON'T SAY IT: YOU GO GIRL

What It Means: female empowerment is a good thing, but "You go girl" is usually the rallying cry for girls who definitely should not go, unless it's to the gym.

It's Only Okay When: followed by, "Seriously. I have to get up early for work tomorrow."

Chapter 2

CHICKTIONARY

(words about women—not that they'll help you understand them)

You don't have to be told that it's impossible to understand women. They're like the universe. We have some theories about why they're here, and we like to look at them through telescopes at night. But just because we don't understand women, doesn't mean we don't need a vocabulary to help us talk about them with our friends.

AMBISEXTROUS *(adjective)*
a combination of bisexual and ambidextrous; when a woman swings both ways sexually.

I didn't know my girlfriend was AMBISEXTROUS when we got together, but I have to admit that it does have some perks.

ARM CANDY *(noun)*
a beautiful woman a man will parade around with so as to show people he's a man of substance, with that substance usually being money.

When his girlfriend figured out the tip before he was done calculating it on his cell phone, he realized she was more than just ARM CANDY.

AUNT FLO *(noun)*
women are fond of saying "my Aunt Flo's in town" as a way to let a guy know she's menstruating, and that he gets to spend the next week appreciating her personality.

The woman in her fifties said that her AUNT FLO is one aunt she's thrilled not to see that often.

DUDE, DON'T SAY IT: AFTER YOU

What It Means: what a pansy says to let someone enter a door ahead of him; the proper term is "ladies first"—even if it's a dude.
It's Only Okay When: it's a single-stall public bathroom, and a trucker has been in there for ten minutes.

BABELICIOUS *(adjective)*
a woman who is so attractive that she can only be described in terms of food.

Only a woman who is totally BABELICIOUS could convince me to quit smoking weed and get a job.

BABY MAMA *(noun)*

a woman who has given birth to a man's child, but with whom the guy is no longer involved.

> He has so many BABY MAMAS that for Mother's Day he just sends a mass e-mail.

BADUNKADUNK *(noun)*

a plump, bouncy female ass.

> Lori took a pretty vicious hit during roller derby, but bounced right back up thanks to her beautiful BADUNKADUNK.

BALL-AND-CHAIN *(noun)*

a wife.

> My wife hates it when I call her my old BALL-AND-CHAIN, but it's what I call her when I'm out with the guys anyway.

> *Well, gotta run. You know how it is, the old **BALL AND CHAIN**.*
>
> CHUCK

 BATTLE AX *(noun)*

a woman who creates so much castration anxiety that the only appropriate term for her is something that both kills and cuts down wood.

I love that my wife got a promotion and makes more money. But the power's sort of turned her into an old BATTLE AX.

BITCH (*noun*)   🏆🏆🏆🏆

a woman who is intelligent, independent, and unwilling to have sex after a man buys her a nice dinner.

My girlfriend wanted me to call her a BITCH in bed, but apparently, she didn't mean in the middle of the night after she's taken all the covers.

BLING (*noun*)   🏆🏆🏆🏆🏆🏆

flashy jewelry; works like fishing lures, except shiny bling is used to get women to jump into a man's boat.

The rapper wore so much BLING that he looked like a Vegas showgirl with bullet scars.

BLUE BALLS (*noun*)   🏆🏆🏆🏆

an extreme nut-sack ache that comes from not being given the opportunity to ejaculate, not even with just a hand job after you promise not to tell her friends.

I've been chasing after this woman for so long that I have BLUE BALLS.

BOOTYLICIOUS (*adjective*)   🏆🏆🏆🏆🏆🏆

describes the large, firm ass of a woman.

It's a good thing Paul's an ass man because his girlfriend is BOOTYLICIOUS.

BOY TOY (*noun*)   🏆🏆🏆

a man who is being used by a woman purely for sex; a happy man.

Bill didn't think things between him and the cougar would last, but he was one happy BOY TOY while they did.

BROS BEFORE HOS *(phrase)*
a reminder to never put a woman before guy friends; best used when one guy is jealous that another is frequently getting laid.

What do you mean you're going to watch the game at your girlfriend's house? BROS BEFORE HOS!

> **BROS BEFORE HOS, man.**
> HUGH LAURIE AS DR. GREGORY HOUSE

BROWN PAPER BAG *(noun)*
a woman who dresses to downplay her attractiveness.

Pete had never really been attracted to Adrienne until he saw her in her yoga pants. Then he realized that she wasn't fugly, just a BROWN PAPER BAG.

BULL DYKE *(noun)*
a lesbian who is so masculine that she's actually a good driver.

The BULL DYKE and I teamed up to hit on a group of girls.

BUTT'ER'FACE *(noun)*
a term used to describe a woman with a great body but less-than-great face. Typically used when explaining why a guy a) did hook up with a butt'er'face or b) didn't hook up with a butterface.

She had a great body, BUTT'ER'FACE . . .

DUDE, DON'T SAY IT: BROTEIN
What It Means: it's both a protein drink, and a very weird term for semen.
It's Only Okay When: explaining to a very beautiful female athlete how you think you can help her diet.

CAMEL TOE *(noun)*
an unfortunate wardrobe malfunction where you can see the outline of a woman's nether regions in a pair of tight pants.

From the back, Lindsey's shorts looked totally killer, but then she turned around and I saw her CAMEL TOE.

CASABAS *(plural noun)*
breasts, especially ones that you have to feel to see if they're ready.

That woman who works in the produce aisle has amazing CASABAS.

CAT CALL *(noun)*
a means by which a group of men boost an attractive woman's self-esteem by making animal-like sounds toward her as she passes by their construction site, so that she knows they would all like to have sex with her.

Thanks for the CAT CALLS, boys. I was having a bad day 'till you objectified me.

CHEAPSKATE *(noun)*
someone who can't ever bring himself to be generous with money, even if it's just to fool a woman into thinking he's generous.

She thought the man in the expensive suit was going to be a sugar daddy, but then she learned that CHEAPSKATE's mom actually bought him the suit because she wanted him to get a job.

CHICK *(noun)*
a woman; chicks come in two varieties: "hot" and "fat."

My friend thinks fat CHICKS and hot CHICKS are one in the same.

CHICK FLICK (noun)

two hours of a man's life that he'll never get back. Chick flicks are typically romantic comedies or tear-jerking love stories.

Bill was rewarded with sex after he bravely sat through the CHICK FLICK without saying, "This sucks!"

CHICK MAGNET (noun)

a guy who easily gets any hot chick he wants—except for lesbians who were born demagnetized.

The CHICK MAGNET loved to pin women up against his refrigerator when they were making out.

CHOCOLATE BUNNY (noun)

someone who is exciting, beautiful, and delicious on the outside but empty on the inside.

I thought my date was the whole package, but when we arrived at the art show and she didn't have anything to say, I realized she was just a CHOCOLATE BUNNY.

DUDE, DON'T SAY IT: CHIC

What It Means: elegant and attractive, especially with regard to clothes; there's only one way men like women's clothes: off.
It's Only Okay When: complimenting a supermodel on the dead bird draped across her shoulders that she's been told is next year's fall fashion.

COCK-BLOCK (verb)

a competitive tactic in which a guy interferes with another guy's attempt to hook up with a girl. A tactic widely employed by player-haters.

I can't believe that dick COCK-BLOCKED me.

COCK TEASE *(noun)*
a woman who leads a guy into believing he will have sex with her, only to leave him hanging.
>That COCK TEASE at work left him with a set of blue balls. Not cool!

COOTIES *(plural noun)*
a parasite found on young girls, which causes the host to chase and kiss boys of the same age. If a boy catches cooties, his friends must make fun of him until the cooties lose all respect for the male host and jump off in disgust.
>My son told his teacher that Sandra gave him COOTIES, so she sent him to the nurse.

DUDE, DON'T SAY IT: COVERLET

What It Means: a bed quilt that doesn't cover the pillows.
It's Only Okay When: you accidentally buy too small of a bedspread and want a fancy name for it.

COUGAR *(noun)*
an older woman who aggressively pursues younger men; characterized by wearing tiger-striped blouses, and frequently mentioning how flexible she still is.
>You wouldn't believe how many COUGARs were at the senior center talent show!

CROCODILE TEARS *(noun)*
fake, insincere crying; like what a woman does so a man will cave and go out with her that night instead of with his friends.
>As the elderly man was being dragged by his foot into the swamp, I saw what looked like CROCODILE TEARS.

DAMSEL IN DISTRESS *(noun)*
a really old term for a woman who is in peril, and needs a guy's help; nowadays it's best used sarcastically when luring a hot chick away from some guy who's interested in a relationship.

It turns out the DAMSEL IN DISTRESS didn't mind that I rescued her from that boring dude at the bar.

DOLLAR MENU *(noun)*
what to order from if you're on a date and there's no chance of getting laid.

The minute she told me she just wanted to be friends, I knew that we'd order dinner off the DOLLAR MENU.

DOMINATRIX *(noun)*
a dominant woman in an S & M relationship; imagine if Martha Stewart was into whipping naked asses instead of soufflés.

I used to date a DOMINATRIX, but one time when I got home from work and said I was beat, she thought I'd cheated on her.

DRAG QUEEN *(noun)*
a man who dresses like a woman on purpose, not because he's from Europe.

All of the DRAG QUEENS could barely contain their excitement upon learning Gillette had come out with a better razor.

> *It's a good thing I was born a girl, otherwise I'd be a DRAG QUEEN.*
> DOLLY PARTON

DRUNK-DIAL *(verb)*
to call a woman while intoxicated, and explain that while yes, you are drunk, you still mean what you say, you love her, no woman compares to her, and that she should come over and bring some condoms.

I DRUNK-DIALED Sabrina last night, and I think we might be engaged.

EYE CANDY *(noun)*
a woman who is so attractive that men can't get past her looks to discover her deep, spiritual nature.

I couldn't get over the amount of EYE CANDY at my girlfriend's family reunion.

> *Yeah, yeah, yeah, that's it. While you were cooking, you know, he was watching one of those, uh, those, uh, telenovels, y'know, with all those ripe honeys on it? Y'know, he was really into it. I told you not to change the channel, man! Y'know, dude needs his EYE CANDY. That's it!*
>
> BREAKING BAD

FUCK BUDDY *(noun)*
a person who has agreed to have no-strings-attached, purely recreational sex with a friend; oddly enough, it's often the women who are willing to just screw that most men find themselves wanting to marry.

I just got a text from my FUCK BUDDY Michelle to meet her at her house in an hour. I guess her date was a bust.

FUGLY *(adjective)*
fucking ugly; best used in emergency situations when one doesn't have the time to say both the words "fucking" and "ugly."

You're drunk, but trust me, she's FUGLY.

FUN BAGS *(plural noun)*

another term for breasts; preferred by men who have objectified women to the point that even thinking of them as produce (casabas, melons) or sources of milk (jugs) doesn't get the job done.

Dude, I'd pay a handling fee for those FUN BAGS.

DUDE, DON'T SAY IT: FANNY PACK

What It Means: a purse that men wear around their waists, and in front of their penises since the wearer of said pack usually is done using his anyway.

It's Only Okay When: figuring out who at Disneyland is obviously European.

GABFEST *(noun)*

an event at which there is entirely too much talking; any conversation between two women.

Unfortunately, the threesome turned into a GABFEST when the two women realized they both went to the same Catholic school.

 GET TOGETHER FOR COCKTAILS *(phrase)*

what women say when they want to get together for drinks and talk about their sex lives.

Bill was so interested about what his girlfriend had to say about him, that when he heard she was planning to GET TOGETHER FOR COCKTAILS, he snuck into the bar and listened in on the conversation.

GIGOLO *(noun)*

a guy who bangs rich women for money.

I tried to become a GIGOLO when I was in college, but none of my ex-girlfriends were willing to serve as references.

GOLD DIGGER *(noun)*
a woman who marries a man just for his money.
The GOLD DIGGER suggested that she and her husband recite their bank-account numbers as their wedding vows.

GRANOLA *(noun)*
a girl who is into eating organic food and wearing weird flowing robes, but makes up for her weirdness by being sexually promiscuous.
This GRANOLA couldn't keep her hands off of me once I told her that I was really into saving the planet.

GREENPEACE *(noun)*
an organization people join to help them feel like they give a shit.
I might join GREENPEACE, because trust fund chicks with underarm hair can be pretty hot.

GRENADE *(noun)*
the ugly girl that you a) either have to hook up with so that your other friends can hook up with her hot friends, or b) a girl so ugly that you have to cock-block your friend from banging her in order to save your comrade.
You owe me a drink, bro. I totally jumped on that GRENADE for you. And she asked me what I'm doing tomorrow. You owe me two drinks!

> *When you go into battle, you need to have some friends with you, so that just in case a **GRENADE** gets thrown at you, one of your buddies takes it first.*
> MIKE "THE SITUATION" SORRENTINO

HASBIAN *(noun)*

a woman who used to be a lesbian, most likely in college.

Susan thought Lena, who she met in her feminist studies course freshman year, was the love of her life, but soon after graduation, Susan learned that Lena was just a HASBIAN.

> That's what we commonly refer to as a *"HASBIAN."*
> THE L WORD

HELLO MOTHER, WOULD YOU LIKE ANOTHER? *(phrase)*

an important way to request sex from a MILF; very often she will want sex, but will not want "another."

So, I said, HELLO MOTHER, WOULD YOU LIKE ANOTHER, but I accidentally called my mom! She said she didn't even want the one she got.

HIGH MAINTENANCE *(adjective)*

a person who needs a lot of time, money, and attention to be happy.

When she learned that I get a spray-on man tan every week she dumped me for being HIGH MAINTENANCE.

> You're the worst kind [of woman]; you're **HIGH MAINTENANCE** but you think you're low maintenance.
> WHEN HARRY MET SALLY

HONEYDEW LIST *(noun)*

a list of all the things a woman expects a guy to do while she's at work, getting a mani-pedi, or gossiping with her friends.

My honey swore up and down that she didn't have a HONEYDEW LIST, but when she went away for the weekend I was instructed to clean the kitchen, rake the leaves, wash the dog, and go grocery shopping.

HOT CHICK (*noun*)
a girl who inspires the desire to have sex, although typically isn't much for conversation.

I asked that HOT CHICK how far she goes on the first date, and she told me that it depends on the traffic.

I LOVE YOU (*phrase*)
what a man says to a woman when he's trying to get her into bed.

I told Maria, "I LOVE YOU" over a bottle of wine.

DUDE, DON'T SAY IT: I'M NEVER HAVING CHILDREN

What It Means: you never want kids, but even if this is true, admitting it greatly lessens your chance for intercourse. The right term is "If I meet the right woman . . ."
It's Only Okay When: a girl says this to you first.

JAILBAIT (*noun*)
a girl that a guy swears he thought was over eighteen, I mean just look at her.

Don't get sucked in by her charms, bro. She's JAILBAIT.

JERK (*noun*)
what a woman calls a man who is honest.

I can't believe you said I'm oversensitive. You're a JERK.

JUGS (*plural noun*)
another word for breasts; comes from "milk jugs" and is the description preferred by men who are mature enough to accept the fact that the things that cause their erections are also capable of feeding a child.

I only like JUGS made from recyclable material.

KEEPER (*noun*)

describes someone worth marrying; for a woman, a keeper is a mature, handsome man with a good job. For a man a keeper is a woman who is great in the sack, and understands that video games are an important part of his life.

When she laughed after I told her what a grenade was, I knew she was a KEEPER.

KINDERGARTEN MATH (*adjective*)
something easy.

If you want to hook up with someone tonight, try that girl at the bar. She's KINDERGARTEN MATH.

KNOCKED UP (*verb*)
pregnant.

We tried to use the rhythm method, but it didn't work; now she's KNOCKED UP and I'm screwed!

By the way, who KNOCKED UP the journalist?
THE LIFE AQUATIC WITH STEVE ZISSOU

LESBO (*noun*)
short for lesbian; best used when a guy is trying to figure out the only plausible excuse for why a woman won't sleep with him.

It's not that I'm forty pounds overweight and unemployed. It's that she's a LESBO.

LIPSTICK LESBIAN (*noun*)
a feminine lesbian.

At first I was confused when I saw that gorgeous woman going out with that manly girl, but then I realized she was just a LIPSTICK LESBIAN.

MAKEUP *(noun)*
creams, powders, and other stuff women apply to their faces to hide their natural beauty.
> No, honey. You don't need MAKEUP. You're beautiful just the way you are.

MAN-CHILD *(noun)*
what a woman calls a man whom she has failed to break of his individuality or desire for happiness.
> My wife calls me a MAN-CHILD just because I refuse to pick up my sex toys.

MENSTRUATE *(verb)*
to have wet underwear mysteriously appear in the sink.
> One of my fantasies is to have a woman be nice while she's MENSTRUATING.

MILF *(noun)*
abbreviation for "mom I'd like to fuck"; refers to a woman who, despite having children, is still smokin' hot.
> I told my girlfriend that her mom's a MILF. But for whatever reason, she didn't take it as the compliment I intended it to be.

DUDE, DON'T SAY IT: MATTE

What It Means: having a dull surface; the problem with this word is that there's an unnecessary "e" at the end.
It's Only Okay When: trying to introduce your somewhat dull friend named Matt.

MILKSHAKE *(noun)*

this term reduces a woman to her fundamentals: "milk" refers to her body, as represented by what her breasts produce, and "shake" describes how sexily she can move her ass.

The way that girl was dancing at the club made me want to put down my beer and get a MILKSHAKE.

MUFFIN TOP *(noun)*

a roll of fat that pushes up and over a pair of pants or skirt that is too tight, or a woman with said roll.

Her MUFFIN TOP made me very uninterested in seeing her muffin bottom.

NYMPHOMANIAC *(noun)*

a woman with an insatiable compulsion for sexual intercourse, cures for which include shock therapy and marriage.

I used to date a NYMPHOMANIAC, but I had to break up with her due to exhaustion.

> **A NYMPHOMANIAC is a woman as obsessed with sex as the average man.**
> MIGNON MCLAUGHLIN

ON THE RAG *(phrase)*

to be menstruating; also may be used as a derogatory way to ask a guy why he's being bitchy.

What's your problem, Terry? Are you ON THE RAG?

PLAY-BY-PLAY *(noun)*
the details; used to discuss topics that a guy's friends will either want to know everything about, or nothing at all.
> Save the PLAY-BY-PLAY on how you met her, and give us the PLAY-BY-PLAY of how you ended up locked out of your apartment in your underwear.

PROMISE RING *(noun)*
a ring teenage girls wear to demonstrate their intention to stay virgins, and home alone every weekend.
> When I see a girl wearing a PROMISE RING, I promise myself not to talk to her.

PURSE *(noun)*
a mobile storage facility that women use to lug around things they absolutely can't leave the house without—such as nail clippers. Also something men are made to hold as a test of obedience.
> My wife always makes sure her PURSE matches my shoes.

DUDE, DON'T SAY IT: PAISLEY

What It Means: a fabric pattern that makes the wearer looks like she's covered in sperm designs.
It's Only Okay When: describing what sperm looks like under a microscope.

PUSSY-WHIPPED *(adjective)*
the mental and emotional conditioning of a man who's being prepared for marriage, characterized by the woman exchanging copious amounts of intercourse for her man's soul.
> Ever since Derek met Veronica he's become so PUSSY-WHIPPED that he never comes over to play Xbox.

> No, wait a minute. You have to "get" the **PUSSY** before you can be **WHIPPED** by it.
> WAITING

RUBENESQUE *(adjective)*
fat but cute—like an overfed cat; men are advised that telling a woman she's fat but cute is no different than telling her she's just fat.
> She didn't begin as RUBENESQUE; she just ate too many Reubens.

SHORTY *(noun)*
pretty girl.
> Hey SHORTY, got any plans for Friday night?

> I roll up on that **SHORTY** be like, "What's up yo?" she be like, "You don't know 20 different ways to make me call you Big Poppa" cuz I don't yo.
> CAN'T HARDLY WAIT

SKEEZER *(noun)*
an overachieving slut or ho.
> The SKEEZER was able to maintain her figure through a strict meth diet.

SLUT *(noun)*
a woman who truly understands what a man needs.
> My ex-girlfriend said you were a SLUT. What are you doing later?

SOCCER MOM *(noun)*
a woman who has traded in her sexuality for a minivan, and spends her days shuttling her kids to various, classes, clubs, and athletic practices.
The SOCCER MOM felt a certain sense of accomplishment as she drove around with a bunch of balls in her trunk.

DUDE, DON'T SAY IT: SPRINKLES

What It Means: Multicolored candy flakes one would use to top ice cream or cupcakes. It's bad enough that you're eating something not made from a dead animal. Adding sprinkles is the culinary equivalent of wearing a dress.
It's Only Okay When: trying to appeal to a MILF by buying her child ice cream.

SPOON *(verb)*
a popular cuddling position in which a man and woman curve themselves around each other as though they were spoons in a drawer.
She likes to SPOON with me, but I wish she saw me more as finger food.

THAT TIME OF THE MONTH *(phrase)*
how a woman tells a man he won't be getting laid for the next week, which he typically doesn't mind since this time of the month is characterized by a woman being very cranky.
In some countries, women stay in a menstruation hut when it's THAT TIME OF THE MONTH.

THIRD DATE RULE *(noun)*
a rule which states that a woman can't have sex with a man until the third date.
Peter knew for sure that he was going to get laid that night due to Liz's THIRD DATE RULE.

TITS *(noun, adjective)*
of course means breasts, but also used by men to describe something as great.

I went surfing today, and the waves were TITS!

> *I do have big TITS. Always had 'em—pushed 'em up, whacked 'em around. Why not make fun of 'em? I've made a fortune with 'em.*
> DOLLY PARTON

TRAILER TRASH *(noun, adjective)*
trailer trash often has no form of entertainment other than sex and, with the abundance of drugs available to her, very often loses all inhibition—thus making her the perfect woman.

I took this TRAILER TRASH chick back to my hotel room. She stole my wallet the next morning, but it was worth it.

TRAMP STAMP *(noun)*
a tattoo on the lower back of a woman.

If my mom gets a TRAMP STAMP, I'm going to change my name.

> *Ah, the TRAMP STAMP. My bread and butter. So I'm guessing that the real story involves a bad breakup and some booze? Unless that's a gang tattoo, in which case I think it's time to find a new gang.*
> HOW I MET YOUR MOTHER

DUDE, DON'T SAY IT: YOU REMIND ME OF THIS CHICK I USED TO KNOW

What It Means: no woman should ever remind a guy of another woman, ever, even if she's her twin sister.
It's Only Okay When: trying to boost a depressed transvestite's spirits.

VAJAYJAY *(noun)*

if anyone should ever doubt Oprah's influence on female society, he should remember that she invented "vajayjay" as a new word for vagina, and now it's real. Men are warned to show Oprah respect; who knows what she might rename our penises!

I knew things weren't going to work out when my date screamed "Stay away from my VAJAYJAY!"

WHAT ARE YOU THINKING? *(phrase)*

the last thing a man wants to hear after sex; however, if a man wishes to have more sex with that female, the right answer is, "How much I like you." If he no longer wishes to have sex with that female the answer is, "That I have to get up early tomorrow."

The great thing about being with two girls at once is that afterward, they can turn to each other to ask, "WHAT ARE YOU THINKING?"

WINGMAN *(noun)*

a friend who helps a guy meet or hook up with a girl.

My brother's a terrible WINGMAN. I told him to say believable-yet-positive things about me, and he told her I was an Olympic gold medalist.

*Iceman: You can be my **WINGMAN** any time.*
Maverick: Bullshit! You can be mine.
TOP GUN

MANWORDS

YES, DEAR *(phrase)*
what a man automatically says to any of his wife's requests; best used when he really doesn't care.

YES, DEAR. I will pick up some milk at the store.

DUDE, DON'T SAY IT: BRIDEZILLA

What It Means: a woman who becomes monstrously bossy leading up to her wedding.
It's Only Okay When: telling your friends that you're about to marry a hundred-foot-tall, green, Japanese chick—who you met while swimming.

Chapter 3

FUEL INJECTORS, FIRECRACKERS, AND FIGHTER JETS

(words for building stuff, destroying shit, and most importantly, doing a half-assed job)

If it weren't for men, we'd all live in pink houses, and wars would be fought by talking shit about the other country behind its back. But fortunately, men built the world. Here are some words with which to talk about our domination—not that there's any reason to talk.

ACADEMIC BULIMIA *(noun)*
cramming facts into your head so you can throw them up the next day for
an exam; most of the time, you won't remember anything you studied five
minutes after you put down your number 2 pencil.

**I used ACADEMIC BULIMIA to graduate from college. The only
problem is that I graduated without really having learned anything.**

 AIRCRAFT CARRIER *(noun)*
a ship on which military planes can take off and land.
**AIRCRAFT CARRIERS rarely shoot, despite being so
full of seamen.**

ANTI-LOCK BRAKES *(noun)*
an automobile braking system that prevents a car's wheels from locking up,
making crashes look far less awesome.

**I installed ANTI-LOCK BRAKES on my kid's bicycle by giving
him new shoes with fresh soles.**

BACKHOE *(noun)*
a tractor used for digging and excavating; it's the only kind of ho for which
a man may remark that his ass hurts after being on it all day.

My BACKHOE came to this country in a shipping container.

BALLAST *(noun)*
this word is primarily used when trying to sound knowledgeable enough in
front of a contractor or electrician so they don't try to rip you off. It is used
to describe anything that provides stability—like a support beam, or a girlfriend with a good job.

**The contractor tried to charge me $3,000 just to install a BALLAST. I
was about to say no, but my girlfriend said she'd loan me the money.**

---

*There is no better **BALLAST** for keeping the mind steady on its
keel, and saving it from all risk of crankiness, than business.*
JAMES RUSSELL LOWELL

MANWORDS

BALLISTIC *(adjective, adverb)*
anything that flies through the air, particularly a bullet. Also anyone who goes crazy is said to "go ballistic." CSI shows love to use the word "ballistic" because it sounds less dumb than "something that goes really fast and hurts."
> We checked the BALLISTICS report. Apparently the guy was shot with a rocket launcher, and that's what made him go BALLISTIC.

BASEMENT *(noun)*
the place in the house where all your shit will end up, provided you can stop your wife from throwing it away in the first place. Basements are also places where men try to invent stuff that they can sell for a million dollars, so they don't have to go to work Monday.
> I went into the BASEMENT to work on that idea for a food rehydrator that I got when I was trying to eat my mother-in-law's Thanksgiving turkey. But I found my old Atari system and played with that for hours instead.

BASS-ACKWARDS *(adjective)*
a scramble of "ass-backwards"; describes something that has been done incorrectly. Best used when criticizing a wife who decided to organize a man cave.
> How am I supposed to go fishing when my lures are all BASS-ACKWARDS?

BIG TIME *(noun)*
a place one finally reaches after years of working one's butt off; while all men want to reach the *big time*, no man should ever ask for directions.
> When Skeeter went from working at quick lubes to changing oil at the Hyundai dealership, we knew he had reached the BIG TIME.

BLINKER FLUID *(noun)*
a mythical product invented by auto mechanics to describe the meaningless services and products they swindle their customers into purchasing.
> **Sorry I forgot to signal, officer. I must be low on BLINKER FLUID.**

BLISTER *(noun)*
a fluid-filled lump of skin; all men should have at least one blister at all times to show that they're hard workers who believe in wearing ill-fitting boots.
> **The manliness my BLISTER gave me dissipated when I cried like a girl when it popped.**

DUDE, DON'T SAY IT: BATH MAT

What It Means: what a woman yells at you to use when you get out of the shower.
It's Only Okay When: you're telling your girlfriend what you've used to remove her dog's dingleberries.

BLUE COLLAR *(adjective)*
designation for a wage-earning worker, whose wage is typically higher than that of a college professor.
> **The BLUE COLLAR worker was kind enough to drop a quarter in the homeless, out-of-work history professor's cup.**

 BOLT CUTTERS *(noun)*
large, plier-looking things that make having a lock's combination or key unnecessary.
> **Instead of buying textbooks, the locksmith's son would just walk through the locker room on the weekends with a pair of BOLT CUTTERS.**

MANWORDS

DUDE, DON'T SAY IT: BROW GEL

What It Means: no guy should care about his appearance enough to know that there's a product for shellacking unruly eyebrows. A woman respects a guy who sports a unibrow that could double as a sun visor more than a guy whose face looks like a woman doing an impersonation of Charlie Chaplin.

It's Only Okay When: you're making fun of another guy with better eyebrows than you. Just be prepared to tell your friends that you learned about brow gel because you accidentally read about it in *Cosmo* while taking a dump at your girlfriend's house.

BUTTRESS *(noun)*

something that props or supports a structure, much the way a fat ass props or supports an even fatter gut.

The noblewoman gained so much weight that her husband started calling her The BUTTRESS of York.

CEMENT *(noun, verb)*

a building material made from water, sand, and gravel. Any man can make cement with materials from the hardware store, and thus he can use it to disappoint a wife who was told she'd be getting a new patio, but was foolishly under the impression that he'd actually hire someone to build it.

The mobster sent his enemy to sleep with the fishes wearing a brand new pair of CEMENT shoes.

CEMENT MIXER *(noun)*

a machine with a revolving drum that mixes cement.

Men love things that make their lives easier; enter the CEMENT MIXER.

CINDERBLOCK *(noun)*
a type of concrete block used for building walls, and also for smashing in karate demonstrations.

> A man who can break a CINDERBLOCK with his bare hands never has to worry about getting his ass kicked by inanimate construction materials.

COCK PUNCH *(noun, verb)*
a punch in the penis; these are the nuclear weapons of hand-to-hand combat, and one should only cock punch if it's going to save more cocks than it hurts.

> I wonder why Ultimate Fighting doesn't incorporate more COCK PUNCHES.

DUDE, DON'T SAY IT: CENTERPIECE

What It Means: something put in the center of the table to make reaching over to grab more food a pain in the ass.
It's Only Okay When: suggesting what your sister-in-law should do with that broken lava lamp you gave her for Christmas.

COMBUSTION *(noun)*
a great word any time you need to describe something that's caught fire or is burning. Mostly it's used for describing standard, gasoline-powered internal-combustion engines. But a guy shouldn't hesitate to tell his friends that after a trip to Vegas, he felt a combusting sensation when he peed.

> Man, that kinda-hot Greenpeace chick from Starbucks won't date me because she says my car has a COMBUSTION engine.

CRANK SHAFT *(noun)*
what a car's pistons turn to make it go; the condition of having an extreme erection due to being high on methamphetamine. In both cases, one runs the risk of throwing a rod.

> The skinny mechanic ogled his friend's CRANK SHAFT.

CROSSBOW *(noun)*
a weapon that can easily be made at home for the purposes of keeping a neighbor's cat out of a man's yard.
> I tried to use my CROSSBOW to take out a squirrel, but I missed and shot a beehive out of a tree.

CROWBAR *(noun)*
a flat, steel bar used for prying open and extracting things— like the truth from a snitch.
> I forgot my CROWBAR at my mom's house, so I had to threaten to beat the rival gang member with a spatula instead.

DUDE, DON'T SAY IT: CRAFTS

What It Means: things women create, often out of pipe cleaners, construction paper, and other items that should only be found in a preschool.
It's Only Okay When: asking your girlfriend if she can turn your old lampshade into a bong.

DENT *(noun, verb)*
to bash something in, or the thing that is bashed in; best used by men to describe having eaten a lot of something.
> Wow, for such a skinny woman you really put a DENT in that pizza.

DESTROYER *(noun)*
a small, fast warship; best used to hunt Somali pirates in paddleboats.
> John won the yachting contest when he entered the bay in a DESTROYER and sank the competition.

DICK AROUND *(verb)*
to sit around and waste time.

> Dude, don't DICK AROUND. We have to leave for the show in ten minutes.

> *You wanna be in a band? Fine. Go ahead. Play every night. Play three times a night! Don't just **DICK AROUND** the same coffee house for five years.*
> REALITY BITES

DIRT *(noun)*
anything filthy; also can mean "salacious details" or a rumor.

> I dug up some DIRT on the man accused of being a grave robber.

DIY *(phrase)*
abbreviation for "Do It Yourself"; refers to massive home remodels, auto rebuilds, or other large-scale projects that a guy thinks he can do himself by just buying some stuff at Home Depot, instead of hiring a professional.

> Four months into his renovation, James turned his DIY project over to a professional.

DONNYBROOK *(noun)*
a fight, particularly among Irish guys named Donny, and usually but not always about some chick named Brook; best used when a man wants to say there was a fight without using a word that sounds violent.

> The situation escalated into a DONNYBROOK when they tried to take my Lucky Charms.

DRYWALL *(noun)*
a common material used in constructing the walls of houses, and a favorite word of contractors trying to explain why they're behind schedule.

> I know it looks like your remodel is far from complete, Mrs. Epstein. But once I hang the DRYWALL it'll practically be done.

DUCT TAPE *(noun)*
a gray cloth tape that men can use for everything from repairing holes in microwave ovens to setting broken arms.

Grandma's having a seizure! Quick, grab the DUCT TAPE.

DUDE, DON'T SAY IT: DAIQUIRI

What It Means: occasionally men must order fruity drinks for a woman so that she can realize she wants to have casual sex; but in order for a man to maintain his masculinity, he must call them "those fruity drinks that come with a straw and shit."
It's Only Okay When: the server doesn't realize that by "fruity drink" you mean daiquiri; then it's okay to quietly mumble, "you know, the *daiquiri.*"

DUMP TRUCK *(noun)*
a truck that can tilt its bed to empty the contents; highly desired regardless of profession, because owning one enables a guy to dump shit onto an annoying neighbor's lawn.

When my neighbor cut down my bushes, I responded in kind and threw a DUMP TRUCK load of manure on his front lawn.

DUMP VALVE *(noun)*
a device that expels excess air from turbo engines; men should appreciate the fact that it basically farts for the engine.

All that diesel fuel made my car's DUMP VALVE work overtime.

EIGHTEEN-WHEELER *(noun)*
a large tractor-trailer whose primary purpose is to shoot rocks onto the windshields of nearby cars.

Guys who drive EIGHTEEN-WHEELERS often piss in empty Snapple bottles and throw them onto the sides of roads.

ELECTRICIAN *(noun)*
an elusive species who for some reason take a week to show up to a house, but when they do arrive, charge $3,000 just for flipping the circuit breaker.

The ELECTRICIAN tried to see how stupid I was by asking if I had extra electricity, or if he should bring his.

DUDE, DON'T SAY IT: INTELLIGENCE

What It Means: the ability to cry over lame shit, or be sensitive to shit that isn't that big of a deal.
It's Only Okay When: explaining to your friends what you're afraid you'll develop if you get fat enough to grow man-boobs.

EXPLOSION *(noun)*
when shit gets blown up.

There was a huge EXPLOSION at the nearby trailer park, and now the cost of meth has tripled.

A horrid alcoholic EXPLOSION scatters all my good intentions like bits of limbs and clothes over the doorsteps and into the saloon bars of the tawdriest pubs.
DYLAN THOMAS

FAMILY BUSINESS *(noun)*
what a guy should say so the person he's ripping off will believe he won't get ripped off because the guy's got traditional values.

My mail-order bride service is a nice FAMILY BUSINESS.

FIRE *(noun)*
The most awesome of all the elements.
When I tried to make Kraft Mac & Cheese, I set the whole kitchen on FIRE.

FLIGHT ATTENDANT *(noun)*
an airplane waitress; previously referred to as stewardesses until they started hiring ugly women, gay men, and gigantic Special Forces guys who bravely defend against future terrorist attacks by handing out pretzels.
If that FLIGHT ATTENDANT wore any more makeup, I'd ask her to perform at my kid's birthday party.

FUBAR *(acronym)*
an abbreviation for "Fucked Up Beyond All Recognition"; originally a military term, but can now apply to anything in disarray.
My hamburger is totally FUBAR because the onions made the bun slide off, and my fingers are covered in ketchup.

FUEL INJECTION *(noun)*
the process by which a car's engine is impregnated with power, through the fertilization of gasoline with air, which then conceives the explosion. It's like getting a woman pregnant, except that your car can't sue for gas money.
I don't believe in FUEL INJECTION before marriage.

GARAGE *(noun)*
every man knows that lawns are for parking your car, and garages are where you store the seventeen-year-old version of yourself, so that your wife can't find it and make it mow the lawn. No garage is complete without a Metallica poster and an old drum set.
Honey, if you want me I'll be in the GARAGE trying to pretend I'm someone else.

GOON *(noun)*
a hired thug or professional ass kicker; men should be advised, though, that when hiring a pack of goons, always do a background check to make sure one of them isn't secretly an intelligent rat or informant.
The hired GOON was so stupid that when he was told to decapitate a rival mob boss, all he did was remove his Yankees hat.

GRAVEL *(noun)*
small rocks are only manly in ginormous quantities, such as with gravel; it is an ideal material for front yards, or for streets that one wishes to drive down while destroying his car's paint job.
The road to hell actually isn't paved with good intentions. It's made of GRAVEL.

GRAVY TRAIN *(noun)*
an unbelievably easy source of money; like if a man got paid to masturbate, and didn't even have to use his own hands.
The celebrity chef's endorsement deals brought him quite the GRAVY TRAIN.

GREASE MONKEY *(noun)*
slang for auto mechanic.
That GREASE MONKEY yelled at that old lady after she refused to also pay for a radiator flush.

DUDE, DON'T SAY IT: GAYDAR

What It Means: the ability to know when someone's gay just by looking at them or the person they're sleeping with.
It's Only Okay When: explaining a feature that comes standard on all Volkswagens.

GUNG HO *(adjective)*
extremely enthusiastic, especially with regard to war.
  When it came to playing *Halo*, the frat guy was always GUNG HO.

HALF-ASSED *(adjective)*
the standard to which all men should strive to do bullshit jobs. Full-assed effort is to be reserved for things men truly care about.
  The fat guy constantly does HALF-ASSED workouts yet expects to lose that full ass.

HANDCUFFS *(noun)*
used by police to restrain a guy under arrest; used by a girlfriend to restrain a guy celebrating his birthday.
  I thought I knew what I was in for when my date HANDCUFFED me to the bed, but I guess I didn't know her as well as I thought I did because she walked out the door with both the key and my flat-screen TV.

HARD-ASS *(noun)*
someone who ruthlessly forces others to follow rules; every hard-ass boss needs a half-assed employee to help them achieve maximum hard-ass-ness; characterized by alternatively being referred to as a "tyrant" or "that fucking guy who just needs to chill out."
  The sumo wrestling coach was a real HARD-ASS when it came to making his wrestlers eat 5,000 calories of rice per day.

DUDE, DON'T SAY IT: HOMOPHOBIA

What It Means: fear of gay people.
It's Only Okay When: explaining why you won't rent *Mission Impossible 3*.

HAZMAT *(noun)*
short for "hazardous materials"; best used when recommending a friend wait before using the bathroom after you.
  I took a job on the county HAZMAT team, but only so I could impress chicks with the hot outfit.

HEADBANGER *(noun)*
either a world-famous rock star, or an unemployed man-child who has long hair, and listens to or plays loud, fast, violent music about Satan, drug abuse, or being angry at one's father.
  The hard-partying old HEADBANGER left his entire estate to his second liver.

HONEY BUCKET *(noun)*
a Port-O-Potty; men are advised that tipping over a honey bucket while a person is inside can lead to serious health risks, and should only be done to a stranger.
  You might catch more flies with honey than with vinegar, but you'll catch even more flies with a HONEY BUCKET.

HOT-WIRE *(verb)*
to start a car without the use of a key; most people can't do this to save their lives, but professional actors can hot-wire vehicles so fast, it's like it's not even real.
  Never HOT-WIRE and steal a soccer mom's car—your getaway music will be all lame-ass kids' songs.

HYBRID *(noun)*
a type of vehicle that runs on a combination of fossil fuel, electricity, and metrosexuality; very valuable to a man who enjoys banging social workers, Trader Joe's employees, or anyone trying to make a difference.
  I know it looks like I'm walking down the street, but really I'm just driving the new HYBRID that's so eco-friendly, only those who truly care about the environment can see it.

I'LL BE THERE BETWEEN EIGHT AND NOON *(phrase)*
a phrase commonly used by cable guys and other home service employees
so that a person will have to miss a half day of work in addition to paying
the cost of whatever they're having done.

> Don't worry, Ma'am. I'LL BE THERE BETWEEN EIGHT AND
> NOON.

DUDE, DON'T SAY IT: I SEE YOUR POINT

What It Means: what a guy says to admit that someone else is
right; the proper male term is, "Yeah? Well fuck you!"
It's Only Okay When: it's cold out and you want to let your girlfriend
know that you can see her nipples.

IMPLOSION *(noun)*
destroying something in such a way that it collapses in on itself, characterized by being totally badass.

> I watched my boss's IMPLOSION from across the desk—and
> chuckled to myself.

INSIDE JOB *(noun)*
a crime committed by employees of the organization that was robbed; not to
be confused with a Senate vote to increase senators' salaries.

> The casino thinks the multimillion-dollar robbery was an INSIDE
> JOB.

JACKHAMMER *(noun)*
a tool designed to break up roads and cause traffic jams. Men like jackham-
mers because they feel like an extension of our own sexuality.

> I wonder if the guy who operates the JACKHAMMER ever feels
> inadequate by comparison?

JOE SIX-PACK *(noun)*

the typical blue-collar guy; so named because anyone who doesn't have a college education goes home every night and drinks beer until he passes out.

I finally got my GED, so now instead of calling me JOE SIX-PACK, I prefer to be called Joe White Zinfandel.

JOIST *(noun)*

typically a long piece of wood supporting either a floor or ceiling. It's important to men mostly because it's typically a long piece of wood.

I don't have a contractor's license. But I've seen several episodes of *This Old House*, **so I'm pretty sure I can install a JOIST.**

KICK-ASS *(adjective)*

should be used when there's nothing subtle about the method or margin of a victory. Such total domination can only be appropriately glorified in terms of striking your foot against another man's rectum.

My new car is so KICK-ASS that I caught my neighbor standing on his front lawn staring at it with lust in his eyes.

DUDE, DON'T SAY IT: KNITTING CIRCLE

What It Means: a group of women who get together to perform manual labor for free; visiting the knitting circle is a special time for women to talk, laugh, and create unwanted Christmas gifts.
It's Only Okay When: describing to your friends what you wish would turn into a daisy chain.

KNUCKLE SANDWICH *(noun)*

slang for a punch in the face; best used when the Subway sandwich artist screws up an order.

Bob got so sick of listening to his staff complain about their lack of a lunch break that he told them he'd order in a few KNUCKLE SANDWICHES.

LANDFILL *(noun)*
ground created from garbage; New Jersey.
> The great thing about living on a LANDFILL is that anytime you throw something on the ground, you're not littering, you're expanding your real estate.

LOCOMOTIVE *(noun)*
what drives a train, be it mechanical or sexual.
> As a kid I thought the caboose was the best part of a train. But as an adult I now know it's the LOCOMOTIVE.

LOW RIDER *(noun)*
a car with specialized hydraulics that allow it to bounce, and get really close to the ground.
> The great thing about hooking up in the back of a LOW RIDER is that the hydraulics do most of the work.

MAKE MINCEMEAT OF *[someone or something]* *(phrase)*
to kick someone's ass so completely that they look like a pile of diced meat.
> Steve's grandma really MADE MINCEMEAT out of him when he said he didn't like her pies.

MAN CAVE *(noun)*
a special place in a house (often in the basement) where men can gather and women are discouraged.
> Come on downstairs, guys. I've got the TV in my MAN CAVE set up for the game. And a keg of beer and pretzels.

> *This is the MAN CAVE, there's no women allowed in here. I got a jerk-off station for God's sake.*
> I LOVE YOU MAN

MELEE *(noun)*
a big-ass fight involving several people, also known as a Polish gang-bang.
A huge MELEE broke out in Vegas when the price of $2.99 steak
and eggs was raised to $3.99.

NAIL *(noun, verb)*
a thin piece of metal used to join two pieces of wood; to have sex with a
woman who was difficult to seduce; best used by a guy to tell his friends
about his weekend.
I thought I really NAILED that date, but she didn't let me NAIL
her so I guess not.

DUDE, DON'T SAY IT: NUT HUGGERS

What It Means: pants or shorts that are so tight they give the man
wearing them a testicular camel toe.
It's Only Okay When: explaining why you refuse to go to the beach
while vacationing in Europe.

NAIL GUN *(noun)*
a pneumatically driven machine that drives nails into stuff; best used when
building a house, or re-creating a scene from a horror movie.
They should update that "If I Had a Hammer" song to "If I Had a
NAIL GUN." If socialists bought better technology, they wouldn't
have to hammer all damn day.

OIL *(noun)*
a viscous fluid that is crucial to powering automobiles, and is also a key
ingredient in the manufacturing of tires, plastics, and wars.
The one good thing about the rising OIL prices is that now it's too
expensive to take my in-laws on that cross-country road trip.

 **PANTS** *(verb)*
to pull down another guy's pants and present his penis to passersby as an act of embarrassment.
Word is that if you PANTS the CEO, he'll give you a huge pay raise.

PIMP *(noun)*
formally, it means a prostitute's manager; also can mean anyone who is a power player.
The PIMP accredits his success to Tony Robbins DVDs, and wearing a ring on his pinkie finger.

> *The way you're dressed, you're either a **PIMP** or a limo driver.*
> BE COOL

PISS BOTTLE *(noun)*
no trucker worth his set of sedentary balls is going to pull over to piss. That's what empty bottles are for.
The rest stop was littered with so many PISS BOTTLES that it made you wonder what the bathrooms were being used for.

PISTOL WHIP *(verb)*
the only thing manlier than shooting a gun is beating someone with the butt of the gun; unlike being pussy whipped, one gains respect if pistol whipped.
I may have earned some street cred by being PISTOL WHIPPED, but it sure didn't help me out in the looks department.

PISTON *(noun)*
a metal cylinder that is propelled up and down by the controlled gasoline fire of a combustion engine; the name of a Detroit basketball team for whom winning NBA championships means its fans propel themselves up and down the streets, setting fires.

The lying-ass mechanic told me I needed to have my PISTONS painted, and said it would cost a thousand dollars.

PLANK *(noun)*
a long, flat piece of wood; even though a plank is technically thicker than a board, men should always use "plank" because it sounds like it should mean something dirty.

My deck is made out of the biggest PLANKS of the hardest wood.

PLIERS *(plural noun)*
a tool that today is used to grasp objects, but was originally used by the Three Stooges to drag people around by their noses.

When she couldn't get the jar open, Maureen resorted to using a pair of PLIERS.

PLUMBER'S BUTT *(noun)*
just as the law requires plumbers to provide a written estimate, so too does it require that they not wear a belt, so that when they bend over, they expose the top third of their ass crack to all the members of your household.

Skinny Steve was kicked out of the union for failing to provide customers with an accurate view of his PLUMBER'S BUTT.

DUDE, DON'T SAY IT: PRODUCT

What It Means: something you put in your hair like mousse, hairspray, or gel.
It's Only Okay When: explaining what makes the back of your hair stand up rather than admitting you have a cowlick and haven't washed your hair in two days.

MANWORDS

PNEUMATIC *(adjective)*

to be powered by compressed air, such as with a nail gun, jackhammer, or flatulent jogger. And like urinating into an empty bowl, the "p" is silent.

My wife was not thrilled with the PNEUMATIC drill I bought her for Valentine's Day, but I thought it was the perfect gift.

POS *(noun)*

short for "piece of shit"; best used when creating a Craigslist ad to sell an old Ford Festiva.

My first apartment was such a POS that I could hear the upstairs neighbor fart.

 **POWER TOOL** *(noun)*

any tool powered by a motor.

My dream is to marry a sexy woman who knows how to operate POWER TOOLS.

PUS *(noun)*

the stuff sores and bruises pee when they've had too much bacteria to drink.

Bill thought his PUS-filled sores would be a nice conversation starter, but he was so wrong.

PYROMANIAC *(noun)*

a guy who loves, and even finds sexual gratification in the setting of fires; women are rarely pyromaniacs because if they wanted gratification from something angry and out of control, they'd just become lesbians.

Moses was the first PYROMANIAC.

RAT *(noun)* 🏋🏋🏋🏋
one who betrays his organization; best used by a mob boss trying to figure out whose fingernails to remove.

The mice gathered to discuss the missing cheese, and the possibility that they might have a RAT.

RAZOR WIRE *(concertina wire) (noun)* 🏋🏋🏋🏋🏋
super badass barbed wire used so passersby could tell the difference between a high school and a prison.

I'm thinking about surrounding my townhouse with RAZOR WIRE to keep the neighbor kids from doorbell ditching.

DUDE, DON'T SAY IT: ROCK OUT WITH YOUR COCK OUT

What It Means: To party so hard that your cock is inadvertently exposed. Note: Your cock should never be exposed while rocking.
It's Only Okay When: you're a headbanger.

REMOTE CONTROL *(noun)* 🏋🏋🏋🏋🏋
a royal scepter, the holder of which has absolute power—and the ability to change channels without moving his ass.

I've been going to night school to learn how to use my foot-long, forty-five-button REMOTE CONTROL.

RETAINING WALL *(noun)* 🏋🏋🏋🏋🏋
a big-ass wall that keeps dirt and shit from filling in a backyard.

I built my house on a jagged beachside cliff that constantly suffers mudslides. But it's okay, because I also put in a RETAINING WALL.

MANWORDS

ROAD RAGE *(noun)*
What a man feels after some moron with his head up his ass cuts him off like he owns the whole fucking road.
> **Some doctors believe ROAD RAGE to be one of the few times men are emotionally honest.**

ROMAN CANDLE *(noun)*
a type of firework that pees sparks into the sky when set on fire; good for Fourth of July celebrations.
> **I think my cat's a communist because it always runs away when we set off ROMAN CANDLES.**

ROUGHNECK *(noun)*
a guy who works on an oil rig or some other tough job; or a really tough guy in general.
> **The ROUGHNECK coal miner's girlfriend was really worried when his shaft exploded.**

SAVVY *(noun, adjective)*
skilled and with understanding.
> **The SAVVY cat knew where the sunbeam would be and so slept there in anticipation.**

SAW *(noun)*
a blade with sharp teeth used for cutting; best used for chasing horny teenagers around a forest.
> **The calluses on my feet got so bad I had to cut them off with a SAW.**

DUDE, DON'T SAY IT: SCRAPBOOK

What It Means: a stupid book or folder filled with magazine cutouts, dried leaves, and other stuff that's supposed to remind a woman of the five times in her life that are actually worth remembering.
It's Only Okay When: explaining to your kids the hobby that led Mommy to save your high school yearbook photo and a condom wrapper.

SCAB *(noun)*

the most masculine form of skin because it's hard, has no feelings, and is often painful to acquire. Also, means someone who has crossed a picket line.

If gotten ahold of by those on strike, the SCAB will probably walk away with a few SCABS.

SCAR *(noun)*

new skin that likes to show off that it took over a part of skin that was previously cut or burned by being discolored or puffy.

My wife was afraid that the cuts from my riding lawn mower accident would leave a SCAR, so she made me go to a plastic surgeon. I went, on the condition that I never had to mow the lawn ever again.

> *The optimist already sees the SCAR over the wound; the pessimist still sees the wound underneath the SCAR.*
> ERNST SCHRÖDER

SCREW *(noun, verb)*

a small, grooved fastener; to tighten either by hand or tool; to have sex.

Wow! That hot contractor really knew how to SCREW.

MANWORDS

SCREWDRIVER *(noun)*
a tool with a thin metal shaft and either a flat or cross-haired point. While originally designed to only tighten and untighten screws, screwdrivers are now used by most men to fix anything ever built.
> Honey, the Blu-ray player won't read the disc. Bring me my SCREWDRIVER.

SHYSTER *(noun)*
a crook, thief, or anyone who underhandedly takes advantage of another.
> I can't believe those SHYSTERS want me to pay extra to check bags.

SISSY *(noun)*
a wimp, especially one who can't or doesn't want to fight; are often fond of saying, "Guys. We can talk this out."
> That SISSY refused to fight his parking tickets in court, despite owing over $1,000.

SLAMMER *(noun)*
slang for prison, and sadly, also is a nickname for smaller men in prison.
> To scare inner-city youths away from a life of crime, the old convict showed them a video of some time he did in the SLAMMER.

SLEDGEHAMMER *(noun)*
a hammer so big it takes two hands to swing it; primarily used for driving railroad spikes and breaking up cement, but can also be used for adding a window to your ex-girlfriend's bedroom.
> The only appropriate tool for slicing a watermelon is a SLEDGEHAMMER.

DUDE, DON'T SAY IT: SNARKY

What It Means: this is a borderline word, but falls within the "words guys shouldn't use" category because it's far more masculine to just be a straight-up asshole than to pussyfoot around an annoyance with biting little comments.
It's Only Okay When: describing a personality trait in a woman that makes you want nothing to do with her.

SLOW HO (noun)
the woman on a construction crew hired to do the all-important job of holding the "slow" sign.
That SLOW HO clearly has never used sunscreen a day in her life.

SMITHEREENS (noun)
itty-bitty pieces; men are advised to always measure power in how thoroughly something can destroy something else.
I hated her 1980s power pop CDs so much that I smashed them to SMITHEREENS.

STREET CRED (noun)
to have respect within an industry or peer group; it's how guys say "respect" without sounding pussified.
The president of the paver's union had a ton of STREET CRED.

STRIPPED (adjective)
when a screw or bolt has lost its thread or teeth; men are advised to always say that something was already stripped, rather than face the potential accusation that they stripped it themselves by using the wrong tool.
Don't worry if the screw is STRIPPED. I'll just use an Allen wrench.

STUD *(noun)*

a supporting beam typically of steel or wood that holds up a structure; a man or animal that's seen as being desirable for breeding.

The mother tree told her lonely son not to worry; one day he'd be a STUD.

STUD FINDER *(noun)*

a tool used in construction to find where the wooden studs are within walls; also, any woman who has good taste in men.

I asked the female Home Depot employee if she had any STUD FINDERS, and she pointed to herself.

DUDE, DON'T SAY IT: SPA DAY

What It Means: a day in which a man's wife leaves in the morning, and then comes back in the afternoon to demand he notice her pedicure.

It's Only Okay When: suggesting where she go to treat herself to something nice—on Super Bowl Sunday.

SUV *(noun)*

short for "sport-utility vehicle," a four-wheel-drive truck with knobby, all-terrain tires; best used by guys who will never spend a single moment driving on anything but paved, city roads.

My wife loves our SUV because it gives her greater visibility of the road she's hogging.

TABLE SAW *(noun)*

a table with a gigantic rotary blade sticking out; when a woman tells a man she wants a new table, this is the only kind he should return with.

We all sat at the TABLE SAW on Thanksgiving, and watched the turkey get carved in fifteen seconds.

TEN-FOUR *(interjection)*
means "Okay, I hear you"; best used when on a CB radio.
> That's a TEN-FOUR, I will be alone for the rest of my life because I'm more into CBs than I am bathing.

THROTTLE *(verb, noun)*
a simpler and manlier way to describe choking the living shit out of some-one; also used to describe the doohickey that controls the flow of gasoline in motor vehicles. If someone uses this word, it means that he either races cars, or lives behind bars.
> The man with anger management issues THROTTLED his son when he found out he'd choked the THROTTLE on his new car.

THUG *(noun)*
a criminal, particularly one who is tough; what a suburban teenager imag-ines himself to be after he steals a pack of gum from the grocery store.
> My mom was such a THUG that she stole the neighbor's bicycle and gave it to me for Christmas.

TITANIUM *(noun)*
an incredibly kick-ass form of metal that is remarkably strong and light; all men are required to own a titanium fishing rod, bicycle, or skull plate.
> Than anatomically correct *Terminator* cyborg went fishing alone just so no one would see him holding his TITANIUM rod.

DUDE, DON'T SAY IT: TEAL

What It Means: a dark greenish-blue found on ducks and for some odd reason on the Jacksonville Jaguars.
It's Only Okay When: describing the most metrosexual color in the spectrum.

TOOL BELT *(noun)*

a specialized belt designed to carry just enough tools so that the pants sag and expose a hairy ass crack.

The things he wanted most in his TOOL BELT were a winning lottery ticket and a beer.

 TORPEDO *(noun)*

to willfully screw something up for another dude; also means "a self-propelled underwater projectile."

The senator's mistress decided to TORPEDO his bid for re-election after he refused to admit the child was his.

TORQUE *(noun)*

something that causes rotation, like a strong wrench or taking a turn too fast in an SUV.

The drunker I got, the more TORQUE the Earth produced.

DUDE, DON'T SAY IT: TISSUES

What It Means: while some men might see tissues as an important bedroom accessory, that usage is outweighed by the box's feminine floral patterns, and a woman's desire to leave boxes of them in every corner of the house.

It's Only Okay When: a man actually has the luxury of spending quality time with himself in every corner of the house.

TRANNY *(noun)*

short for both "transmission" and "transsexual." A man should be careful if asked if he knows how trannys work. It might be an inquiry to fix a car, or for a date.

My mechanic thinks I might be looking at a new TRANNY, and said I should come back tonight so he can pop the hood. He also said I should bring my car.

TYRANT *(noun)*
one who uses his or her power oppressively; best used when describing any human who asks a man to do anything he doesn't want to do.
I can't believe that TYRANT asked me to wash my hands after I used the bathroom. It's not like I'm making *his* sandwich.

VANILLA *(adjective)*
boring, run-of-the-mill.
When we were dating we had tons of hot, dirty sex. Now everything that happens in the bedroom is just plain old VANILLA.

> *VANILLA? I'm not VANILLA. I've done lots of crazy things. I mean I got drunk and married in Vegas.*
> FRIENDS

VELCRO *(noun)*
a type of fastener for shoes and wallets. It is the least manly way to keep something closed, and therefore should be made fun of if seen in use by someone other than a toddler.
I don't care if he is a black belt. I'm pretty sure I could take any man that uses a VELCRO wallet.

VIOLENCE *(noun)*
what all movies and TV shows must have if they are to be watchable. Violence is judged on a spectrum of funny, like watching Adam Sandler get kicked in the nuts; to totally awesome, like in *Gladiator,* during that first battle scene when Russell Crowe throws a phone at Germania.
The VIOLENCE alone in *Roadhouse* is so awesome, it almost makes you forget you're watching a movie starring Patrick Swayze.

WALKIE-TALKIES *(noun)*

wireless two-way communication devices that men appreciate for their ability to let them talk to another guy without having to actually be near him.

My wife complained that we never talk, so I bought a set of WALKIE-TALKIES.

WATTS *(plural noun)*

a unit of electrical power; men should keep in mind that to discuss the number of watts produced by something they own, is to discuss penis size as though it were measured in the ability to light a house.

I've got a 4,000-WATT amplifier that's so powerful that when I play my guitar, my upstairs neighbor has an orgasm.

DUDE, DON'T SAY IT: WEDDING FAVORS

What It Means: little useless pieces of shit given out to members of a wedding party.

It's Only Okay When: asking if, instead of the lame-ass picture frame or travel clock, you can take the bridesmaid as your wedding favor.

WEDGIE *(noun)*

having underwear wedged up your ass, normally caused by being someone's younger brother.

One time I was given such a deep WEDGIE that my underwear looked like it had tire treads.

You know, kids, a lot has changed since your old Uncle Joker's been away. New Gotham, new rules, even a new Batman. But now I'm tanned, I'm rested, and I'm ready to give this old town a WEDGIE again!
BATMAN BEYOND: RETURN OF THE JOKER

WIRE *(noun)*
a device placed on an informant that allows him to record illegal activity; if one is ever wearing a wire, it's important to take a piss so the surveillance team in the van can listen in disgust.

I don't believe he's an electrician! See if he's got a WIRE.

WORKING STIFF *(noun)*
a guy who is stuck in a boring yet necessary job.

Even though people thought the gigolo had a wild job, he just thought of himself as another WORKING STIFF.

ZONE OUT *(verb)*
to stop paying attention, to daydream.

Our date was going well earlier in the evening, but when she starting talking about her sister's kids, I totally started to ZONE OUT.

People look at me and they get bored, people listen to me and they ZONE OUT . . . bored. "Who is that boring person?" they think. "I've never before met anyone so boring."
HAPPINESS

Chapter 4

SHNOCKERED, SMASHED, AND SHITFACED

(words to know when you wake up drunk with a penis drawn on your face)

Alcohol plays a very important role in the lives of men. For starters, it allows us say things to each other that would be considered weird otherwise. It also helps us bond (remember, bros before hos, man). And when men drink or party too hard, less-than-attractive women get laid, which turns ordinary dudes into penis-wielding humanitarians. Here's the lexicon for when you get your drink on.

ACID *(noun)*
a hallucinogenic drug; a chemical capable of eating through metal and other solid substances. Acid is either manufactured in a laboratory, or found in the circulatory systems of people who party too hard.

One time I took so much ACID that I thought Lady Gaga was attractive.

If God dropped ACID would he see people?
STEPHEN WRIGHT

ALCOHOL *(noun)*
any intoxicating liquid that helps men both celebrate life and confront its challenges.

What's a bachelor party without ALCOHOL? There's no better way to send a bro off to the altar than totally wasted.

ANGRY DRUNK *(noun)*
that friend who wants to fight when he gets drunk; men can spot the angry drunk as the out-of-shape guy who rips his shirt off and says, "What, motherfucker? You gotta problem?!"

I knew Paul was an ANGRY DRUNK—and a moron—when he went after the bouncer who was three times his size.

BAKED *(adjective)*
high on marijuana; it should be noted that "frying" is slang for being high on acid, and marijuana enthusiasts will always argue that baked is healthier than fried.

Last night I was so BAKED that I sat on the counter for a half-hour to cool off.

BEER *(noun)*

what 80 percent of the Earth would be covered in if God were really a man; the only thing invented in the Middle East more valuable than algebra.

I drank so much BEER last night that I told my wife I loved her.

BEER BELLY *(noun)*

a fat stomach as a result of drinking a lot of beer; a sign of male maturity. Unlike the man who has six-pack abs and is trying to please women with his appearance, the man with the beer belly clearly does not give a shit what other people think.

My BEER BELLY keeps me warm in the winter.

BEER BONG *(noun)*

a funnel connected to a hose that helps the user rapidly get really drunk; best used when you're late for work and don't have time to drink a twelve-pack in the traditional manner.

The girl with a high booze tolerance had trouble getting drunk, so she used a BEER BONG to speed up the process.

DUDE, DON'T SAY IT: BFF

What It Means: short for "Best Friends Forever"; the proper male term is, "I've known that dude a long time."
It's Only Okay When: asking an attractive woman if her BFF wouldn't mind taking a cab home. If she's a real BFF, she'll do it.

BEER GOGGLES *(noun)*

a fictitious set of "goggles" that men wear as they get drunk, with the magical ability to make a female who more closely resembles a horse somehow seem attractive enough to fold down the backseat of a car and take home.

He must have had BEER GOGGLES on when he went home with that chick.

BENDER *(noun)*
to drink for as long as it takes.

    When Jeffrey's mother told him that she's a lesbian, and that his father used to be a woman, he went on a two-week BENDER.

BINGE DRINKER *(noun)*
a man who finishes what he starts, especially if he's starting to develop cirrhosis of the liver.

    Maybe I was a BINGE DRINKER in college, but now I wake up with a hangover from just a six-pack and a rum and Coke.

DUDE, DON'T SAY IT: BUGGER

What It Means: a sodomite.
It's Only Okay When: telling an Englishman to piss off, or when you're trying to remember the name of the guy your wife hired as an interior decorator.

BLACKOUT *(noun)*
what occurs when you've drunk so much that you forget large portions of your evening, and perhaps even your life, forcing you to rely on friends to tell you how much of an ass you were.

    I don't remember starting a dumpster fire last night. I must have had a BLACKOUT.

BLOW THE BOWL *(verb)*
to accidentally cough while smoking weed through a pipe, blasting the burning hot ganja embers all over your friend's parents' carpet.

    She BLEW THE BOWL for the second time that night. If there wasn't something else I also wanted her to blow I would have kicked her out.

DUDE, DON'T SAY IT: BRONZER

What It Means: A spray-on fake tan. If you're not willing to develop basal cell carcinoma, then you're not man enough to have a tan.
It's Only Okay When: telling friends why one of the girls at the beach looks like she was tagged by a graffiti artist.

BLUNT *(noun)*
a cigar that's been hollowed out and filled with marijuana.
I was very direct in explaining how to roll a BLUNT.

BODY SHOT *(noun)*
when a chick puts salt somewhere on her body, holds a lime in her mouth, and then the guy does a shot of tequila, licks the salt/her body, and takes the lime/kiss; the perfect combination of booze and heavy petting.
Mike thought he was dreaming when the tall blonde asked him to do a BODY SHOT.

BONG *(noun)*
a long, cylindrical tube that is used for both smoking weed and as an inversely proportional measure of a guy's sperm count and future job prospects.
I got this awesome new five-foot BONG! You have to stand on a ladder to smoke from it.

 BOOZE CRUISE *(noun)*
a boat trip with the specific purpose of getting drunk; best used on spring break.
On the BOOZE CRUISE, my girlfriend got drunk, puked over the side, and attracted some of the most beautiful tropical fish I'd ever seen.

CHIEFED *(verb)*
to have people draw shit on a guy after he passes out drunk; best done with permanent ink, and on a friend who has a family function the next day.
My friend who binge drinks is always getting CHIEFED; you'd think he'd learn his lesson.

DUDE, DON'T SAY IT: COLONIC

What It Means: to have your anus washed like one would hose out the dirty corner of a garage.
It's Only Okay When: telling a doctor what men don't need.

COLD TURKEY *(adverb)*
a sudden cessation of having fun, as opposed to entering a twelve-step program or rehab where you stop doing something gradually.
When Jim made up his mind to quit playing *World of Warcraft* COLD TURKEY, he realized that girls like guys who actually leave the house to socialize.

CRUNK JUICE *(noun)*
typically some combination of an energy drink and hard liquor; best served from a gas can.
I was supposed to take my girlfriend out on a date later that evening, so to stay alert I told the bartender to just keep pouring me CRUNK JUICE.

CRUSH HOUR *(noun)*
last hour a bar is open to find someone to go home with for the night.
By the time CRUSH HOUR came around Will was starting to feel so desperate that he tried to get it on with that soccer mom in the back of her minivan.

DESIGNATED DRIVER *(noun)*

the one friend who agrees to stay sober in order to drive; a side benefit of being the designated driver is witnessing how obnoxious drunk people can be.

I was the DESIGNATED DRIVER, which means the night sucked.

DOUBLE FISTING *(verb)*

holding on to more than one drink at a time; a technique commonly used at weddings with an open bar.

I had to drive Dave home because he was DOUBLE FISTING all night.

DUDE, DON'T SAY IT: CURVES

What It Means: suburban weight-loss centers.
It's Only Okay When: telling your girlfriend what you like about her.

DRUNK SEX *(noun)*

to have sex while remarkably intoxicated.

I only knew that I'd had DRUNK SEX because when I woke up, I saw a bra on my floor, and a new number in my phone.

 DRUNK TANK *(noun)*

where one wakes up if he's been arrested with a DUI during his blackout.

When I woke up in the DRUNK TANK, I knew that I was about to spend the next year taking the bus to work.

EAT THE WORM *(verb)*
to drink a particular type of tequila that comes with a pickled worm at the bottom; men are advised that it is the only time "eat the worm" can sound masculine.
I was told my mom and dad met when he dared her to EAT THE WORM.

FRANKENFOOD *(noun)*
genetically modified food; best eaten when heavily intoxicated.
I'm sure the fast food I'm eating could be considered FRANKENFOOD, but it's so delicious that I don't care.

FRAT HOUSE *(noun)*
a place where young men puke off balconies and penetrate coeds; also a derogatory description of any dwelling in which there are too many dudes wearing volleyball visors.
The FRAT HOUSE threw a party to celebrate their combined 4.0 GPA.

 GANJA *(noun)*
marijuana; contrary to popular belief, this word isn't Jamaican but actually comes from ancient Hindi; best used to explain why a tech support guy keeps laughing at a caller's questions.
When I smoke GANJA I can hear God, but he always just tells me to order a pizza.

GNAT'S PISS *(adjective)*
a way of describing a beverage with either a weak flavor, or low alcohol content; best used by alcoholic foreigners who can't seem to get a buzz from American booze.
The German entomologists considered American beer to be GNAT'S PISS.

MANWORDS

GRASS *(noun)*

marijuana. Stoners can best be broken into two camps: those who see life as growth and wonderment—who thus prefer to call it grass; and those who see everything as a hassle that ultimately gets in the way of them getting high—who prefer to call it weed.

I like to smoke GRASS, but it makes dieting a bitch.

HAIR OF THE DOG THAT BIT YOU/ME *(phrase)*

alcohol that is consumed the next morning to lessen a hangover.

I was going to just have a little HAIR OF THE DOG THAT BIT ME, but I ended up drinking the whole damn dog.

DUDE, DON'T SAY IT: HUG IT OUT

What It Means: how one guy offers to hug another, either to comfort, or to end an argument.
It's Only Okay When: used sarcastically, as in, "Oh wow, I feel so bad for you that that hot chick only slept with you twice. Wanna hug it out?"

HAMMERED *(adjective)*

drunk to the point of sounding as intelligible as a man who was bludgeoned with a hammer; best used for bragging to friends about how close a man came to death.

Dude, I was so HAMMERED last night that I told Jane what an asshole her boyfriend was when I was standing right in front of him.

HANGOVER *(noun)*

the process by which the universe collects the fun you had last night so as to make sure life stays on a continuum of average; characterized by puking, and praying to God that you'll never drink again.

Last night was so fun. But I woke up with a HANGOVER that made me wish I'd stayed home.

> *I feel like I have a **HANGOVER**, without all the happy memories and mystery bruises.*
> ELLEN DEGENERES

HAPPY DRUNK *(noun)*
a person who is happy when intoxicated; these people are often miserable when not drunk, and so should be encouraged to stay drunk at all times.

Kim is a HAPPY DRUNK; too bad it's the only time she's fun to be around.

HOUSE PARTY *(noun)*
when half of a guy's school or college comes over to get drunk.

I actually found a beer in my mom's knitting bag after my HOUSE PARTY.

I WAS DRUNK *(phrase)*
a frequently used excuse to explain activities as diverse as throwing a brick through a storefront, to having sex with a girl who, if sober, a guy would ask to free Han Solo.

Dude, I don't know how that tiger ended up in your parents' bedroom. I WAS DRUNK.

DUDE, DON'T SAY IT: IT'S COMPLICATED

What It Means: The details are so complex that it's not worth explaining. Anything not easily explainable is not worth being involved in.
It's Only Okay When: explaining to your wife why you don't want her checking your Internet browsing history.

JÄGERMEISTER *(noun)*
a particularly clever type of alcohol that disguises how much one has drunk until it's too late.
> It's not my fault that I drove the car into your pool! I had too much JÄGERMEISTER.

JELL-O SHOT *(noun)*
Jell-O that's been made with vodka instead of water.
> Since it was a kid's party, all the adults decided the right thing to do was have JELL-O SHOTS.

JOINT *(noun)*
a marijuana cigarette; the intersection of two body parts, such as the wrist to the hand, or the hand to the mouth when smoking a joint.
> I find that smoking a JOINT relieves my JOINT pain.

JUNGLE JUICE *(noun)*
a drink in which a ton of hard alcohol is mixed with Kool-Aid or random fruit juices.
> I drank so much JUNGLE JUICE that I tore my clothes off and covered my body with leaves—too bad it was poison ivy.

KARAOKE *(noun)*
the art of annoying the shit out of people in a bar by singing out of tune with a favorite song.
> I'll go to KARAOKE with you, Brenda. But if you sing any Britney Spears or Justin Bieber, you'll have to find a new ride home.

KEGERATOR *(noun)*
a refrigerator converted to house a keg of beer; a bold statement that shows how a man correctly prioritizes cold beer over fresh vegetables.
> Nothing turns a house into a bachelor pad like a KEGERATOR.

KEGGER *(noun)*
a party whose main attraction is kegs of beer; men should be advised that some women are intimidated by the thought of attending a kegger, so to get a woman to the gigantic party where she'll no doubt drink to the point of losing all sexual inhibition, be sure to refer to it as a "little get-together."
She seemed like a prude, but once we got to the KEG-GER she started flashing anyone who'd fetch her a beer.

KEG STAND *(verb, noun)*
to do a handstand on a keg and drink while upside down; best done when a man wishes to combine gymnastics with binge drinking.
My deltoids and liver are sore from doing KEG STANDS last night.

LUSH *(noun)*
a person who is such an alcoholic that they seem blessed with a rich, dense forest of broken relationships and health problems.
My gardener is a total LUSH.

> ## DUDE, DON'T SAY IT: LEAVE-IN CONDITIONER
>
> **What It Means:** hair conditioner that one does not rinse out, and which provides silky, soft, perfect hair that a woman deserves to have. A real man's hair, on the other hand, must be so brittle and lifeless that a strong breeze should blow it off the scalp like a tumbleweed.
> **It's Only Okay When:** explaining to your wife why your showers are ten minutes long.

MEDICAL MARIJUANA *(noun)*
incredibly potent marijuana sold at dispensaries by stoners who know what they're doing.
You cannot get a prescription for MEDICAL MARIJUANA unless you have a valid medical reason, such as an ingrown toenail or a really sore pimple.

MICROBREW (*noun*)
a beer produced from a local brewery in small batches and with limited distribution; best drunk when needing to appear hip.
I want to create a MICROBREW that goes international.

MOONSHINE (*noun*)
illegal homemade whiskey with dangerously high alcohol content.
For some reason my mama would celebrate all my birthdays by drinking MOONSHINE with my uncle.

> *Well, between Scotch and nothin', I suppose I'd take Scotch.*
> *It's the nearest thing to good **MOONSHINE** I can find.*
> WILLIAM FAULKNER

MYSTERY BRUISE (*noun*)
bruises that are acquired either during strenuous labor or intense drinking, and of which the bruisee isn't aware until he looks down and says, "Holy shit. Where did that bruise come from?"
The MYSTERY BRUISE on my shin and my broken bicycle led me to believe I must have done some BMXing while drunk last night.

NARC (*noun*)
anyone who will tell parents or the authorities about someone's underage drinking or weed smoking; best used trying to keep a younger brother from tagging along to a party.
You can't go, Jon. I know you, and you'll NARC me out to Mom and Dad if you see me drinking or smoking weed.

PACKIE (*noun*)
liquor store.
John was pissed when the PACKIE ran out of his favorite white zinfandel.

> *My hand to God: there is a **PACKIE** in Salem and Peabody, Mass., that's called Bunghole Liquors. You can't make that shit up.*
> THE IMPROPER BOSTONIAN

PADDY WAGON *(noun)*
a form of public transportation especially reserved for intoxicated and unruly people.
> I never take cabs home. Since I live near the police station, I just cause trouble 'till the PADDY WAGON arrives.

DUDE, DON'T SAY IT: PEN PAL
What It Means: a person who is too far away to actually care about, but for some reason is frequently written to.
It's Only Okay When: trying to impress an English major with your penis's pet name.

PARTIED-OUT *(adjective)*
a rarely achievable state during which a guy has partied so hard that he no longer wishes to party; being partied out can last from a few days to a few years depending on how hard the person used to party.
> The first time I peed pure malt liquor is when I realized I might be PARTIED-OUT.

PARTY CRASHER *(noun)*
a guy who shows up to a party he wasn't invited to; can mean both an actual person who shows up when not invited, or anything that's unwanted.
> I was all excited for the third date, but then her Aunt Flo became a PARTY CRASHER.

PARTY FOUL (*noun*)
dropping a beer, puking in the living room, or doing something that brings a party to a screeching halt.
  Billy checked the rule book, and calling the cops as a prank is definitely a PARTY FOUL.

PARTY POOPER (*noun*)
a person with the amazing ability to ruin any fun event just by being himself/herself.
Oddly enough, the bingo parlor only allows PARTY POOPERS.

DUDE, DON'T SAY IT: PASTEL

What It Means: soft crayon-type things used for sketching annoying pictures of sunsets and homelands; often characterized by muted pinks and purples, which create amazing surreal images of the "My Little Pony" world the artist wishes she lived in.
It's Only Okay When: trying to describe what the desert at Burning Man looked like when you were really stoned.

PIE-EYED (*adjective*)
drunk to the point of looking like you're squinting, but not so drunk you can't use a two-syllable word to describe how blasted you are.
  I'm not PIE-EYED, officer! I just lost a contact.

PISS DRUNK (*adjective*)
a degree more intoxicated than "shitfaced," and a degree less than "wasted"; while it can mean a drinking session in which a man was so drunk that he pissed in, on, or around something (including himself) not normally pissed in, on, or around; it can also just mean really drunk.
  Mike knew he got PISS DRUNK last night when he woke up face-down on the bathroom floor.

PLASTERED *(adjective)*
wasted; incredibly drunk.

Jim got so PLASTERED when he was working on his house last weekend that the plaster on the wall was all a total disaster.

 POLLUTED *(adjective)*
so drunk that people declare you off limits.
I threw beer cans into the river so I could get the fish totally POLLUTED.

PONY KEG *(noun)*
a half-sized beer keg that holds about 62 pints of beer—about enough to last a couple of guys an evening.

Hey, man, wrestling's on the tube tonight and you've only got a PONY KEG for five of us? You're gonna have to hit a package store in an hour.

DUDE, DON'T SAY IT: PUMICE STONE

What It Means: a volcanic rock women use to soften bunions and calluses; a task just as easily accomplished with a cheese grater or belt sander.
It's Only Okay When: inquiring why your girlfriend's bathtub looks like it had just been in a meteor shower.

POT HEAD *(noun)*
a guy who loves marijuana so much, it's the only thing he thinks about.

That ceramicist is a total POT HEAD.

PUB CRAWL *(noun)*
a fantastic event where you roam from one bar to another having at least one drink at each one.
I went on a PUB CRAWL with my wingman and we must have had a great time because I didn't remember anything the next morning.

RAGER *(noun)*
a big, crazy party at which serious drinking occurs; best used to describe some of the funniest high school experiences, as well as where you got that scar.
Before they built all those houses, it was just a field where we'd have RAGERS.

REEFER *(noun)*
marijuana; best used when trying to tell a person from the 1950s why your cereal tastes so good.
Man, let's go up to the roof and smoke some REEFER.

REVERB *(noun)*
an effect applied to sound that makes it echo, usually created by a specialized amplifier, or really good mushrooms.
I can't tell if Phish is using REVERB, or if I'm just trippin' balls.

DUDE, DON'T SAY IT: RAINBOW

What It Means: diffracted light, that's all.
It's Only Okay When: asking why the guy at work with the rainbow bumper sticker never wants to hit the strip clubs after work.

ROLLING PAPERS *(plural noun)*
papers that, if found by their teenage owner's parents, will be claimed to be materials for a school project—which is to get high.
The Amsterdam customs official asked to see my ROLLING PAPERS.

SHNOCKERED, SMASHED, AND SHITFACED   107

ROOFIES *(noun)*
a type of medicine that cures a woman of not putting out; if caught putting a roofie in a woman's drink, a man can go to prison and might be subjected to acts for which he'll wish he could take a roofie.

When he woke up in the cougar's bedroom, he knew that either ROOFIES had been slipped in his drink or he had been way too drunk.

SAUSAGE FEST *(noun)*
a party with too many guys and not enough women.
Dude, this SAUSAGE FEST is totally lame. Let's hit a strip club.

SHINDIG *(noun)*
a small party; best used when just trying to invite close friends to a get-together.

I told Betty I was having a little SHINDIG, but when she arrived I then said everyone else had to cancel, but there's no reason we should let the case of beer go to waste.

SHITFACED *(adjective)*
a level of drunkenness in which a man has droopy red eyes, a puffy face, and generally looks like shit.

Matt rescheduled his job interview because he had gotten SHIT-FACED the night before and his face was still showing the aftereffects.

SHNOCKERED *(adjective)*
so drunk that a guy can't even say "snookered" without slurring.
I just pissed myself. So yeah, I guess I'm SHNOCKERED.

SHROOMS *(noun)*

short for magic hallucinogenic mushrooms; when a guy is high on mushrooms, it is one of the few times he is permitted to describe something he doesn't plan to screw as beautiful.

I took so many SHROOMS that I actually felt like calling my mom just to talk.

SLOSHED *(adjective)*

so drunk that one feels like beer sloshing around in a barrel; almost always used in the past tense, because anyone currently sloshed wouldn't be able to pronounce it.

I was so SLOSHED last night that I peed on the sofa—while standing on the coffee table.

DUDE, DON'T SAY IT: SPANDEX

What It Means: a super-elastic fabric worn by women who like to exercise, and men who like to have their balls stared at.
It's Only Okay When: laughing at people wearing Spandex.

SMASHED *(adjective)*

drunk to the point of feeling broken; often when people wake up with mystery bruises after a hard night of partying, those bruises are from being smashed.

When my girlfriend asked me where that mystery bruise came from, I told her it must have happened when I got SMASHED at the party last night.

STEWED *(adjective)*

so drunk that your insides slosh around like they were potatoes, carrots, and celery.

I wouldn't have eaten that chili if I had known I was going to get STEWED.

STICKY WEED *(noun)*
particularly potent marijuana that has an adhesive-like quality.
That STICKY WEED did nothing but stick my ass to the couch.

STONED *(adjective)*
so high on weed that one sits on the couch exhibiting physical movement
and brain activity similar to that of a stone.
**My dad said that he was so STONED when he met my mom that
he at first thought she was a Martian spying on Earth as a Denny's
waitress.**

> *Do you think God gets STONED? I think so . . . look at the
> platypus.*
> ROBIN WILLIAMS

STONER *(noun)*
a guy for whom being high is an essential part of his being; while stoners
are often excellent as a companion with which to play video games, they are
typically terrible roommates.
**What happened to that guy? He used to be a total STONER, and
now he showers every day and has a job. It's a shame.**

TANKED *(adjective)*
best used to warn a friend that he's too drunk to drive. Since it comes from
the term "drunk tank," the knowledge might somehow penetrate his inebriated skull that he could end up in one if he drives. Tanked is a degree less
drunk than "shitfaced" and one higher than "sloshed."
**I was pretty TANKED last night, but I think I'd remember running
from the cops.**

TECHNICOLOR YAWN *(noun)*

particularly colorful projectile vomit, often caused by having eaten candy or doing Jäger Bombs.

My wife filmed my TECHNICOLOR YAWN with our new hi-def camera, and I can't wait to show off the picture quality at this year's Thanksgiving.

THE MUNCHIES *(noun)*

a condition in which someone who has just smoked a ton of weed craves food, and will eat anything and everything, and a ton of it.

I had THE MUNCHIES so bad that I put cut-up hotdog on my ice cream.

THE SQUIRTS *(noun)*

liquid diarrhea that is often caused by drinking too much; it doesn't help that while drunk, many men eat food that alone would give them the squirts.

Please let yourself in! I have a bad case of THE SQUIRTS and can't get to the door right now.

TRIPPIN' BALLS *(verb)*

to be so high on drugs that you must add the word "balls" as a sort of testicular exclamation mark.

If you lick this frog, you'll soon be TRIPPIN' BALLS.

TRUCKER SPEED *(noun)*

over-the-counter uppers, typically ephedrine, that real men use when the world can't wait an extra day for its shipment of frozen pizzas.

Scientists are conducting studies to see if TRUCKER SPEED leads to an increase in speeding tickets.

TWEAKER *(noun)*
a person fond of speed and meth; if you have a tweaker in the family, it's important to get him help—right after he's finished cleaning your bathroom.
> That crazy TWEAKER grabbed and twisted my nipple!

UPCHUCK *(verb)*
to throw up; best done in the bushes of the neighbor's house.
> I thought no one would find out that I UPCHUCKED in my neighbor's garden, but I forgot they had a dog.

DUDE, DON'T SAY IT: UNICORN

What It Means: an ideally beautiful, mythical horse that women love because it flies around with a single, giant, phallic horn on its head.
It's Only Okay When: strapping on a dildo to fulfill your wife or girlfriend's *real* unicorn fantasy.

VALIUM *(noun)*
also called "Mommy's Little Helper," it's a sedative that has narcotic qualities and can allow someone to get drunk on much less booze.
> My mom said she started taking VALIUM after I was born because with the extra mouth to feed, she needed a way to cut her booze budget.

WASTED *(adjective)*
pretty damn drunk.
> Dude, he is so freakin' WASTED!

> *I never thought I was WASTED, but I probably was.*
> KEITH RICHARDS

WASTOID *(noun)*

a guy who has chosen to be in the brain-cell extermination business (i.e., taking drugs).

> When the investment banker lost his job, he became a total WASTOID.

WILD CARD *(noun)*

the person in the group who makes the night exciting by doing some crazy shit.

> Gary thought last night was going to be boring, but then our WILD CARD showed up.

> *Because I cut the brakes! WILD CARD, bitches! Yeeeee-haw!*
> IT'S ALWAYS SUNNY IN PHILADELPHIA

WINO *(noun)*

an alcoholic who favors wine over other types of booze, presumably because life feels less out of control when one tries to match his addiction to fish or beef.

> The WINO prefers cabernet, but he's really not all that picky.

DUDE, DON'T SAY IT: JASMINE

What It Means: a favorite of scented-candle makers, jasmine fills the air with a sweet, tropical smell, and sets a perfect mood for a woman to spend the evening pleasuring herself in the bathtub.
It's Only Okay When: it's the name of a stripper.

YACK *(verb)*

to talk incessantly, or to vomit; often done in succession by a drunk chick or dude at a party.

> Jack YACKED in his backpack, and that's a fact.

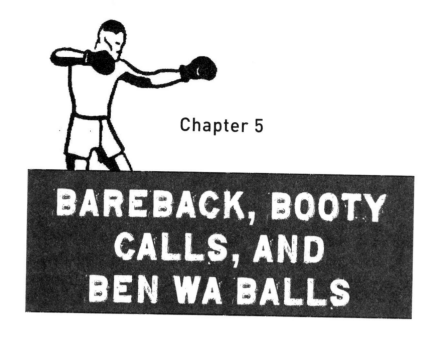

Chapter 5

BAREBACK, BOOTY CALLS, AND BEN WA BALLS

(important sex terms and innuendos for when a man meets that special whatever-her-name-is)

Any woman will tell you that sex is a very important part of a relationship. But any man will tell you that a relationship is a very important part of getting sex. The only thing as important to men as getting laid is finding the most creative way to describe it to our friends.

ADULT *(adjective)*
a way to make "pornographic" sound less dirty.
> The man was arrested after walking into the ADULT bookstore, and asking the clerk where the Young Adult section was.

ALARM CLOCK *(noun)*
a woman who wakes you up for sex.
> Ever since Melissa and I started dating, I have been exhausted. She is a total ALARM CLOCK.

DUDE, DON'T SAY IT: AROMATHERAPY

What It Means: the use of smells to make people feel better—because nothing cures paranoid schizophrenia like a honey-scented candle.
It's Only Okay When: you're explaining to your wife why you farted in line at Bed Bath & Beyond. It may not have made those around you happier, but it improved your mood, and that qualifies as aromatherapy.

AUTOFELLATIO *(noun)*
the ability to self-administer fellatio. Technically, it's a form of masturbation. But practically, it's gross.
> The yogi trained for years to achieve enlightenment and AUTOFELLATIO.

BALLS-DEEP *(adjective)*
to really get thoroughly into something.
> I could have spent the night with Veronica, but I chose to be BALLS-DEEP in poker night instead.

BAREBACK *(adverb)*
to have sex without a condom. Going bareback is very special and should only be done with a woman you love enough to accidentally get pregnant.

That girl I hooked up with last night begged me to go BAREBACK, but I'm not ready to be some chick's babydaddy.

BAZONGAS *(plural noun)*
tits so big that only an invented word can describe them.

There's no way that waitress's BAZONGAS are real.

BEAT OFF *(verb)*
to masturbate.

I wonder if Michael Jackson used to BEAT OFF to "Beat It."

 BEN WA BALLS *(usually plural noun)*
a string of various-sized balls that women use to strengthen their vaginal muscles, increase sexual pleasure, or to place in a man's anus for extraction at the time of orgasm. Also called vaginal beads, because if a woman wants a foreign object stuck in her vagina, naturally it would be jewelry.

I was wary of trying BEN WA BALLS, but I started calling them "ben wow balls" after what happened last night.

BLOW JOB *(noun)*
something men don't get after they say "I do."

When we hooked up I thought I was going to get a BLOW JOB, but then I remembered that we were married.

> *Life is like a permanent limp dick, with an occasional **BLOW JOB**.*
> LARS ULRICH

BOINK (*verb*)
to have sex, either on a bouncy surface or in a bouncy woman.
> I know it was kind of dirty, but we BOINKed in the bouncy house after the kids' party.

BOOTY CALL (*noun*)
like telemarketing, except that instead of a product, the offering is impromptu sex, and there will definitely be no long-term contracts.
> I got a 2 A.M. BOOTY CALL from my ex-girlfriend's best friend, which goes to show that the best advertising is word-of-mouth.

> That's what a girl wants to hear: "Darling, do all the weird crap you like, just don't be late for the BOOTY CALL."
> VERONICA MARS

BROTHEL (*noun*)
like a McDonald's for sex, except that you might want to avoid the ones with signs saying, "Over a billion served."
> I never expected to end up at a BROTHEL for my bachelor party.

BUBBLE WRAP (*noun*)
the goosebumps some women experience before orgasm.
> I knew Mary was getting close when I felt her BUBBLE WRAP.

BUMPING UGLIES (*verb*)
to have sex; never to be said to the woman whose uglies are actually being bumped; most women like to think all parts of their body are beautiful and respected.
> When I asked the overly sensitive woman if she wanted to BUMP UGLIES she broke down in tears.

BUSH *(noun)*
pubic hair.
> The botanist had a great BUSH.

BUST A NUT *(verb)*
to ejaculate or something equally as awesome.
> Dude, don't BUST A NUT. They haven't even made it to the Super Bowl yet.

DUDE, DON'T SAY IT: BOOK CLUB

What It Means: a group of people who gather to talk about books because their health insurance doesn't cover group therapy.
It's Only Okay When: explaining what an old lady needs in addition to her cats to pretend to have a fulfilled life.

CAPTAIN AMERICA *(noun)*
Like the comic book Captain America who always has his shield at the ready, this dude always has a condom set to go.
> Ever since my girlfriend's pregnancy scare I've become a real CAPTAIN AMERICA.

CASANOVA *(noun)*
a nicer way of saying that a guy's a slut.
> Mark used to be a real CASANOVA, and he's got the Valtrex prescription to prove it.

 CHASTITY BELT *(noun)*
a belt worn by medieval women that prevented sexual intercourse; the original cock blocker.
> It's rumored that Paris Hilton wears a CHASTITY BELT just because she enjoys making her boyfriend pick the lock.

CHI CHIS *(plural noun)*
Mexican term for breasts.

> That cheap bastard took his date to Taco Bell and then tried to touch her CHI CHIS.

DUDE, DON'T SAY IT: CONNECT ON AN EMOTIONAL LEVEL

What It Means: women are big on trying to get a guy to connect with them on an emotional level. Beware! This is the psychological equivalent of holding a chick's purse.
It's Only Okay When: telling a woman what she needs to hear so that you can then connect on a physical level.

COITUS *(noun)*
to have sex; useful if a man's going to try to bang a hot college professor, or has invented a time machine and is planning a sex-vacation to the Roman Empire.

> When the intellectual asked me if I wanted to go back to her place and engage in COITUS I jumped at the chance.

CONDIMENTS *(plural noun)*
originally a term used to describe ketchup, mustard, and other things you'd put on a sandwich, but now used to refer to condoms.

> That chick at this party is into me. Do you have any CONDIMENTS I can borrow in case we go out to eat later?

CONDOM *(noun)*
the thing in a man's wallet assuring that he won't get laid.

> I always let women know there's a CONDOM in my wallet. That way, they know they aren't wasting their time talking to me.

> *A **CONDOM** is the glass slipper for our generation. You slip one on when you meet a stranger. You dance all night, and then you throw it away.*
> FIGHT CLUB

COOCHIE *(noun)*
vagina.
> She didn't really care for the fact that I called her vajayjay a COOCHIE.

CUPCAKE *(verb)*
to stay in and cuddle instead of going out.
> Michael was pissed when Rebecca wanted to CUPCAKE instead of going to his brother's frat party.

DILDO *(noun)*
a robot penis; all women own them and men should be no less offended by the fact that their competition is twice their size than a woman should be that the porn stars men fantasize about have gigantic breasts and tiny waists.
> My girlfriend's DILDO keeps the home fires burning when I'm out of town.

> *Mac: You are such a **DILDO**, dude.*
> *Dennis: Thanks, dude, thanks. That's a good way to start the day.*
> IT'S ALWAYS SUNNY IN PHILADELPHIA

DOES THE CARPET MATCH THE DRAPES? *(phrase)*
used when asking if a woman's pubic hair is the same color as the hair on her head.
>After I banged the hot redhead, my bro asked me, "DOES THE CARPET MATCH THE DRAPES?"

DOGGIE-STYLE *(adjective)*
a sexual position that is especially courteous for women, as they can be pleasured without having to stare at a man's contorted O-face.
>I'm cool with my wife wanting to do it DOGGIE-STYLE, I just wish she didn't want to do it in the backyard in front of the neighbors.

DOIN' THE NASTY *(phrase)*
to have dirty sex.
>She told me not to shower, because she couldn't wait to start DOIN' THE NASTY.

DUDE, DON'T SAY IT: EUROTRASH

What It Means: a fashion trend in which guys wear tight shirts and shoes without socks—because nothing complements a great physique like the smell of toe jam.
It's Only Okay When: explaining to a date why you aren't wearing socks, other than the fact that you haven't washed your whites in two months.

DRY HUMP *(verb)*
when a man and a woman simulate sexual motion while fully clothed; it's about as fun as fucking laundry.
>She insisted that she and her boyfriend only DRY HUMP because she wanted to wear white on her wedding day.

MANWORDS

ELOPE *(verb)*
to run off and secretly get married.
> After hearing about her wedding plans I asked her if she wanted to ELOPE.

ENERGIZER BUNNY *(noun)*
a sexual partner who takes what feels like forever to orgasm.
> All I wanted to do was go to sleep, but my ENERGIZER BUNNY just kept going and going.

 FLOG THE DOLPHIN *(verb)*
to masturbate.
> I only FLOG THE DOLPHIN when there's no tuna in my net.

FLUFFER *(noun)*
a person who makes sure male porn stars are either prepared with boners, or maintains their boners in between takes; also used to describe anyone or anything meant to help in some sort of preparation.
> The FLUFFER'S favorite sandwich is a fluffernutter.

FRIENDS WITH BENEFITS *(phrase)*
two friends who have sex, but aren't in a romantic relationship.
> I was all about being FRIENDS WITH BENEFITS, but when Carol started to want flowers and expensive dinners, I called everything off.

> *You'll be happy to know that I now have a much better understanding of "FRIENDS WITH BENEFITS."*
> THE BIG BANG THEORY

GETTING ONE'S POLE SMOKED *(phrase)*
to receive oral sex.

When Tom went to the barbeque he certainly didn't expect to GET HIS POLE SMOKED.

GLORY HOLE *(noun)*
a hole in a bathroom wall, typically at a truck stop, through which a man may stick his penis for some anonymous fellatio.

Even a one-night stand is better than using a GLORY HOLE.

HAND-JOB *(noun)*
the minimum sexual concession a woman will make when she's not in the mood but he is.

Despite the fact that she "had a headache" she offered to give me a HAND-JOB.

HANKY-PANKY *(noun)*
having sex with a woman when a man should be focused on something more important—like having sex with two women.

They said what I smelled was a new aromatherapy candle, but I could swear I walked in on some HANKY-PANKY.

HAPPY ENDING *(noun)*
a hand-job received after a massage.

The massage was great, but I was disappointed when the spa didn't offer a HAPPY ENDING.

> *So, Nurse Gandhi-rella, I need you to suction this guy, do a wet-to-dry dressing change, and, oh, what the hell, go ahead and top him off with one of your special, special sponge baths. HAPPY ENDING optional—his choice, not yours.*
> SCRUBS

HERMAPHRODITE *(noun)*
a person with both male and female sex organs; it's like getting a fortune cookie with two fortunes—one of which says that "sometimes it's wise to keep secrets."
I don't care how big a HERMAPHRODITE'S breasts are. They can never compensate for also having a penis.

 HIDE THE SALAMI *(phrase)*
to have sex.
The Italian magician loved to play HIDE THE SALAMI.

HIT THAT *(verb)*
to have sex.
Man, what I wouldn't give to HIT THAT.

HORNY *(adjective)*
turned on or sexually primed: you can tell when a woman's horny because her vagina's wet and her nipples are hard. And you can tell when a man's horny because he's awake.
Susan was so HORNY that she had sex with a guy who was wearing a fanny pack.

HUMMER *(noun)*
getting a blow job by a woman as she hums; a truck that sucks gas typically driven by dicks.
When gas prices hit $3 per gallon, I was worried I was going to have to start giving HUMMERS to gas up my HUMMER.

IN-LAW SEX *(noun)*
sex that has to be quiet so your in-laws sleeping down the hall don't know what's going on.
I thought IN-LAW SEX would be a snooze-fest, but boy was I wrong!

KAMA SUTRA *(noun)*
an old Hindu sex guide.

> I accidentally got my kids a copy of the KAMA SUTRA because I heard it had pictures of elephants.

LANDING STRIP *(noun)*
a popular female pubic hairstyle inspired by modern aviation.

> I followed my girlfriend's LANDING STRIP right into the terminal.

DUDE, DON'T SAY IT: HELLO KITTY

What It Means: a brand of stationery and purses that are so feminine that the pencils automatically dot every "I" with a heart.
It's Only Okay When: trying to help foreign exchange students feel at home.

LIBIDO *(noun)*
the sex drive; men are advised that not all women have high libidos, and before dating it's best to have a woman fill out a questionnaire regarding how often she would like to do it.

> Nothing throws a woman's LIBIDO into high gear like taking her to a wedding.

DUDE, DON'T SAY IT: LINENS

What It Means: sheets, towels, or any household cloth that a man improperly folds.
It's Only Okay When: you've run out of toilet paper, and need to ask your wife which of her linens she loves the least.

LOVE 'EM AND LEAVE 'EM *(phrase)*
a nicer way of saying "pump and dump"; best used in a Match.com profile to explain what kind of a relationship the man's looking for.
His LOVE 'EM AND LEAVE 'EM philosophy helped him save a lot of money on flowers.

LUBRICANT *(noun)*
used to make a vagina capable of being comfortably penetrated—that is, if a guy's standard forty-five seconds of foreplay have somehow failed to make the female wet.
She asked if I would kiss her for a while, and I asked, "Why? Are you out of LUBRICANT?"

MACK *(verb)*
to let a lovely lady know that you're interested.
That bitch tried to MACK on Lisa's fiancé, so she stared her down.

> *Ronald McDonald proved to be a huge flirt with all the women at the clown retirement home. In fact, they called him the Big MACK.*
> DAME EDNA

MASTURBATE *(verb)*
to stimulate oneself to orgasm; best used when filling out the "hobbies" section of a job application.
For some reason, I like to MASTURBATE while talking to tech support; it's kind of like phone sex.

DUDE, DON'T SAY IT: MANOREXIA

What It Means: it is the male version of anorexia—any guy who ever hears the word "manorexia" directed toward him needs to put down the meth and go eat a pizza.
It's Only Okay When: your wife or girlfriend even looks at a guy who's skinnier than you; in that case it's appropriate to accuse the guy of having manorexia.

MEAT MARKET *(noun)*
a bar at which men and women congregate for the sole purpose of finding someone with whom they can have meaningless, awesome sex.
>I tried to get laid at a MEAT MARKET, but every woman told me I was past my expiration date.

MÉNAGE À TROIS *(phrase)*
three people having sex; what a man tells his girlfriend he wants right before they break up.
>My girlfriend said we could finally have that MÉNAGE À TROIS, but when I got to her house, her ex-boyfriend was there. That wasn't what I had in mind.

MOJO *(noun)*
charisma; luck with the ladies.
>I totally thought I was in with that hot chick, but she turned me down. I must have lost my MOJO.

DUDE, DON'T SAY IT: MAUVE

What It Means: a purplish color.
It's Only Okay When: showing a woman the part of your body that turns mauve when excited.

O FACE *(noun)*

the face one makes when having an orgasm.

John wished that he hadn't installed the mirror above his bed when he saw his O FACE.

> I'm thinking I might take that new chick from Logistics. If things go well I might be showing her my *O-FACE*. "Oh . . . Oh . . . Oh!" You know what I'm talkin' about. "Oh!"
>
> OFFICE SPACE

ONE-NIGHT STAND *(phrase)*

when a man and a woman have sex, and then never see or call each other ever again.

It was just a ONE-NIGHT STAND. She said she likes me, but not in a "want to admit to anyone she slept with me" kind of a way.

ORGASM *(noun)*

sexual climax, characterized by ejaculation if a male, and having a petit mal seizure followed by an annoying desire to cuddle if a female.

She said I gave her such a good ORGASM that it was almost like being with her vibrator.

PASTIES *(plural noun)*

small adhesive nipple coverings; worn by strippers so as not to be indecent.

Sometimes a woman wearing PASTIES is hotter than one who isn't. Guys like a little mystery after all.

POCKET POOL *(noun)*

when a guy rubs his penis and balls through the pocket in his pants; best used when being fitted for a tuxedo.

My penis always tricks me by getting hard at the last moment—because it's a POCKET POOL shark.

DUDE, DON'T SAY IT: OVULATE

What It Means: when a woman lays her eggs, and then sends them from the nest.
It's Only Okay When: breeding pit bulls.

POON TANG *(noun)*
a word that objectifies the female sex organ to make it sound like it's some southern delicacy that should be served with grits.

Will can't help himself; he goes crazy every time someone opens a can of POON TANG.

PULL OUT *(verb)*
a method of birth control in which a man removes his penis from the vagina hopefully before he ejaculates. If he thinks he might've ejaculated even a little bit in the vagina, it is male custom to lie and say he didn't.

No. I absolutely, 100 percent PULLED OUT in time. I swear.

DUDE, DON'T SAY IT: PILATES

What It Means: a bunch of stretches women do to fool themselves into believing they've actually exercised; if men wanted to sit on the floor while trying to bend their heads to their nuts, they could do that in the privacy of their own homes.
It's Only Okay When: you want to get to know the Pilates instructor, and maybe see if you can surprise her with a few stretches she doesn't know.

PUMP AND DUMP *(verb)*
a term referring to a guy having sex with a girl, and then breaking up with her. This is usually done because the guy likes the girl so much that he can't take how real his emotions are, and so just has sex with her to deny how much he really likes her.

Man, I felt bad, but I had to PUMP AND DUMP. She wouldn't stop talking.

QUEEF *(noun)*
a catastrophic release of air from a vagina during or after sex. They are known to destroy boners in a matter of seconds.
She QUEEFED and then started giggling. That's when I remembered I was late for work.

QUICKIE *(noun)*
really hot, quick sex that can go from start to finish in under a minute—instead of the traditional four minutes.
My wife said she wanted more than a QUICKIE, so I also rented a movie.

DUDE, DON'T SAY IT: QUICHE

What It Means: an omelet pie; it's actually quite tasty, but the problem is that quiche is usually served at fancy B & B's . . . and you don't want to get dragged to one of those.
It's Only Okay When: you're a famous celebrity chef. It's okay to eat lame-sounding food if you're rich and famous.

RHYTHM METHOD *(noun)*
a method of accidentally impregnating a woman by not having sex on those days when a woman guesses that she's at an infertile window in her ovulation cycle.
The RHYTHM METHOD only works if you also use a condom.

 ROADHEAD *(noun)*
to get a blow job while driving; men are advised that during roadhead it is highly advised to slow down for speed bumps.
I had a dream that I was receiving ROADHEAD, but it turned out that I just fell asleep with a warm laptop on my crotch.

RUB ONE OUT *(verb)*
to masturbate; best used to describe the masturbation one does prior to a date so that, in the event of intercourse, the guy doesn't prematurely explode.
> **I know I have feelings for a woman when I need to go to the restaurant's bathroom during dinner to RUB ONE OUT.**

SEX *(noun)*
when a man and woman care about each other, the man puts his penis into her vagina and moves it 'till he ejaculates, and she shakes and clenches simultaneously; or when a man and woman are married, the guy shuts his eyes and pretends she's the slutty-looking bank teller, and he's her gynecologist.
> **Dry humping only counts as SEX if walking past a jewelry store counts as buying an engagement ring.**

SEXPERT *(noun)*
a person who is an expert at doin' the nasty.
> **The cougar said she'd train me to become a SEXPERT.**

SEXTING *(verb)*
to text-message nude photos or receive nude photos via text message; a double-edged sword for men because, while it allows guys to show their friends what they've had sex with, it also makes it tougher to lie about what they've had sex with.
> **This girl keeps SEXTING me, but all of her pictures have red-eye.**

SHAG *(verb)*
to have sex with; best used when bedding a British chick.
> **I once SHAGGED a chick on a shag carpet. It was groovy.**

DUDE, DON'T SAY IT: STEMWARE

What It Means: wine glasses; real men only drink from bowls like a dog.
It's Only Okay When: explaining what that crash was.

SINGLE-MOM SEX *(phrase)*

the passionate, thrilling intercourse that can only come from a woman who understands that her single-mom status means that every time she has sex might be her last—and usually understands this every weekend with someone new.

That woman who bought me drinks took me into the back of her minivan, and gave me the best SINGLE-MOM SEX of my life.

SIXTY-NINE *(noun)*

a sexual position in which a man and woman have their heads simultaneously buried in each other's crotches; best used when a man wishes to show a woman that he cares about her just as much as she cares about him.

She kept saying that I was only interested in my own happiness, so to show her it wasn't all about me I flipped her over for a little SIXTY-NINE.

SLOPPY SECONDS *(noun)*

the act of hooking up with someone after that person has already had sex or a relationship with someone else.

When I started dating Joe's ex he wouldn't let me forget that I was just eating up his SLOPPY SECONDS.

> So what's up? You got a friend for Silent Bob, or are you just gonna do us both? If so, I'm first. I hate **SLOPPY SECONDS**.
> *DOGMA*

 SPANK THE MONKEY *(verb)*

to masturbate. These days most experts see spanking as a form of mistreatment, and instead recommend giving the monkey a timeout.

The primatologist was fired for SPANKING HIS MONKEY.

> *In a world gone mad, we will not SPANK THE MONKEY, but the monkey will spank us.*
>
> *JAY AND SILENT BOB STRIKE BACK*

SWALLOW *(verb)*
what a woman of quality and substance does to show a man she really cares.

When she didn't SWALLOW, I knew I wasn't ready to change my Facebook status to "in a relationship."

SWITCH HITTER *(noun)*
a person who is bisexual.

When my wife found out I was a SWITCH HITTER, she let me know that she didn't have any team loyalty either.

SYMPATHY SEX *(phrase)*
to have sex with someone as an act of charity; men should be advised that with regard to sympathy sex, 'tis just as good to give as to receive.

That was the fifth woman this month who gave me SYMPATHY SEX when I told her my dog died. Had I known, I would've pretended to have a dead dog years ago.

DUDE, DON'T SAY IT: STRESS EAT

What It Means: to overindulge in food; men are advised to stress drink since developing a beer belly is more widely acceptable for men than growing a fat ass.
It's Only Okay When: explaining why it makes sense to put a Baskin-Robbins next to a fertility clinic.

TADPOLE *(noun)*
a guy who dates cougars.
> The cougar didn't mind dating the TADPOLE because she knew one day he'd grow up to be a frog prince.

TEABAG *(noun)*
when a gentleman repeatedly dips his testicles into a woman's mouth.
> When TEABAGGING, men are advised to be courteous, and ask the woman if she takes one lump or two.

TOSS OFF *(verb)*
to masturbate; especially a session in which the man's semen sets a new Olympic long-jumping record.
> I wasn't planning to TOSS OFF this morning, but I accidentally saw my hot neighbor bend over to pick up her newspaper.

VIBRATOR *(noun)*
a vibrating sex toy; contrary to popular belief, it makes a woman orgasm not because of its inhuman abilities, but because she trusts it.
> Before my business trip, I bought my wife a VIBRATOR, to which she said she'll still probably swing by the neighbor's house to borrow batteries.

 WALK OF SHAME *(noun)*
when a person wearing the clothes he or she wore out the night before heads home after a one-night stand with the person he or she picked up at the bar/restaurant/truck stop.
> I spent the whole morning at what's-her-name's apartment because I was too hungover to take the WALK OF SHAME sooner.

> Hey look, it's my mom doing the WALK OF SHAME . . . out with the guy you met on a porn site?
> ONE TREE HILL

WAR WOUND *(noun)*
injury imparted during sex.

> Ariel gave Chris a hickey last night and he wore a turtleneck to hide his WAR WOUNDS.

WRAP IT UP *(verb)*
to use a condom.

> If a girl's Facebook picture is her holding a bottle of vodka, you'd better WRAP IT UP if you're going to hit that.

DUDE, DON'T SAY IT: WRINKLE CREAM

What It Means: fancy lotion that a woman uses to try to reverse time.
It's Only Okay When: trying to come up with a way to charge $30 an ounce for hand lotion.

WHAM-BAM THANK YOU MA'AM *(phrase)*
how a gentleman thanks a lady for a quick act of sex during which the woman typically forgoes her opportunity to have an orgasm.

> The woman crushed my self-esteem when, after I said, "WHAM-BAM THANK YOU MA'AM," she said it's *no big deal.*

Chapter 6

STRAIGHT BALLIN'

(words every man needs to talk about sports, especially valuable for professional athletes who were only required to take DNA tests in college)

Men need something to do when they're not fighting or having sex. Enter the wonderful world of sports. Sports play an important role in male bonding, and help young people develop important trash-talking skills that will allow them to either talk their way out of a situation or get their ass kicked for the rest of their lives. It doesn't matter if you're a baller, a surfer, or a NASCAR nut. No dude worth his dodgeballs should be without the following:

ACHILLES HEEL *(noun)*
where a man is vulnerable (if there were such a place).
His ACHILLES HEEL is that he thought he had an Achilles heel.

ACL *(noun)*
abbreviation for "anterior cruciate ligament," the part of the knee that, when torn, makes athletes suddenly suck. Sportscaster guys like to say "he tore his ACL" because it sounds smarter than, "he fucked up his knee."
I knew if I drafted the quarterback onto my fantasy team the guy would tear his ACL.

DUDE, DON'T SAY IT: ATOMIZER

What It Means: the thing that turns liquid perfume into a fine mist so that when sprayed, nearby men can choke and have their eyes water.
It's Only Okay When: you use one to light flammable liquids, and create big clouds of fire.

AMATEUR *(noun, adjective)*
someone who is not yet a professional, or a professional who behaves unprofessionally.
That meeting with all the new recruits was a total AMATEUR hour.

ARMCHAIR QUARTERBACK *(noun)*
a guy who, despite never having played a down of professional football in his life, still knows enough about what a quarterback's doing wrong to criticize him; also, anyone who thinks he's an expert in a subject he actually doesn't know shit about.
The commissioner of my fantasy league was a real ARMCHAIR QUARTERBACK.

ATV *(noun)*

abbreviation for "all terrain vehicle"; a very fun yet remarkably dangerous means of traveling though rivers, up mountains, and eventually, to heaven.

When my brother bought his son an ATV for Christmas, his neighbors could hear his wife screaming at him.

 BALL PARK *(noun)*

a place where a guy takes his kids so drunks can teach them new curse words; more generally used to inquire if a guy has a shot at something, or if two people are in agreement.

I asked the female golfer what she was doing later, just to see if I was even in the same BALL PARK. She said we weren't even in the same sport.

BALLER *(noun)*

a very successful man, especially a professional athlete or a rapper.

Lance Armstrong is not the BALLER he once was.

BALLS-OUT *(adverb)*

a term used to describe using all of your resources to achieve a particular goal. Clearly if a man is willing to have his balls out, he isn't worried about suffering pain or future consequences.

Carl really went BALLS-OUT on his new nudist resort enterprise.

BANANA HAMMOCK *(noun)*

Speedo.

Are you seriously wearing a BANANA HAMMOCK? Dude, you're not a professional swimmer, get a pair of board shorts already!

BASE JUMP (verb)
parachuting off of objects, instead of jumping out of an airplane; because any man knows that there's no point in living unless you're continually increasing your chances of dying.

David was going to BASE JUMP from the top of the Eiffel Tower, but instead he pussed out and spent the day eating crepes, *éclairs*, and *boeuf bourguignon*.

BIG SHOT (noun)
a very important person.

Back in the day lighting my farts made me quite the elementary school BIG SHOT.

BITCH TITS (noun)
breasts grown by a guy on steroids.

It's worth having BITCH TITS if it means turning pro.

BLITZ (noun, adjective)
a defensive football play in which many of the defenders abandon their coverage assignments and instead try to kill the quarterback; also used to describe anything that can knock a guy on his ass.

The linebacker famous for blitzing quarterbacks has just been BLITZED by several paternity suits.

BOBBLEHEAD NIGHT (noun)
when professional baseball teams have a promotional event at which all of the attendees get a plastic caricature of a star player; some are so lifelike they even say "I did not use steroids" when you pull a string on their backs.

Normally, I wouldn't go to a baseball game, but it's BOBBLEHEAD NIGHT, and I need some random shit to put on my desk at work.

BOWLING *(noun)*
a game in which smokers try not to hack up a lung while tossing a ball at a bunch of pins.
The Professional BOWLING Association has recently banned oxygen as a performance-enhancing substance.

BUFFED *(adjective)*
to be so muscular that women are almost as attracted to you as they are to gay guys.
I thought getting BUFFED would get me laid, but it turns out there's no size bicep that compensates for living in your mother's basement.

CADDY *(noun)*
a guy who carries your shit for you on a golf course, and pretends he knows the course well enough to help improve your game. Also useful as a person to blame for having a bad round.
I kept asking my dumbass CADDY which club he thought was best, and he kept saying Studio 54.

DUDE, DON'T SAY IT: CINEMA

What It Means: not to be confused with Cinemax, which is a cable channel specializing in soft porn, "cinema" is a fancy word for movies that try to make the viewer feel and think. The only time men should feel and think is when playing strip poker.
It's Only Okay When: you're watching foreign cinema that has a lot of gratuitous sex under the guise of being a love story. It is okay for a man to be a fan of any cinema that makes him hard.

CANNON *(noun)*
slang for a really strong throwing arm, particularly that of a quarterback.
The quarterback's black eye proved that his two-year-old son had a CANNON for an arm.

CHARLEY HORSE *(noun)*
cramps are what women get on days when they call in sick to work. When a man's muscle cramps, he gets a charley horse. The name comes from a famous horse named Charley who once was not given enough Gatorade following a derby.

I never thought I could get a CHARLEY HORSE from playing Wii bowling, but it turns out that I was wrong.

> *It's like a CHARLEY HORSE in the back. It's better than it was. I couldn't skate right now, but maybe (today). It all depends on how quickly I heal.*
>
> TODD FEDORUK

CHEERLEADER *(noun)*
a young woman who uses her sex appeal to sell enthusiasm for a group of men; best used when bragging to friends about the girl you're dating.

No one was surprised when the head CHEERLEADER married the quarterback the year we graduated from high school.

CLOBBER *(verb)*
to beat the crap out of someone; best used to describe sports, physical violence, or other forms of nonsexual male entertainment.

That Chow mix CLOBBERED the competition at the dog show.

CONTRACT DISPUTE *(noun)*
when a professional athlete is angry at the club he plays for, because he believes he should get several more millions of dollars per year than the millions he currently earns.

I used to work as a professional dart player, but had to quit over a CONTRACT DISPUTE.

DUDE, DON'T SAY IT: CREPE

What It Means: an ultra-thin pancake; the only things that thin that a guy should consume are edible undies.
It's Only Okay When: telling a French chef what his food tastes like.

CRACK-BACK *(noun)*

a particularly brutal type of football block in which an offensive player basically blindsides a defender, and knocks him on his ass.

> That was an illegal CRACK-BACK! Where was the ref on that play?

CROTCH ROCKET *(noun)*

a very fast, loud motorcycle; a penis.

> All it took to get her to go out with me was a ride on my CROTCH ROCKET.

 CYCLIST *(noun)*

a man who trades two testicles for two wheels.

> I was considering becoming a professional CYCLIST, but then my wife told me she wanted to have kids.

DUDE, DON'T SAY IT: CROCHET

What It Means: a type of needlework that produces hats, handbags, and even nauseatingly adorable tissue-box cozies.
It's Only Okay When: receiving a crochet golf-club cozy. It looks like a homemade scrotum, and is therefore acceptable.

DIVOT *(noun)*

a chunk of golf course.

> I thought I was going to be a great golfer, but then I looked behind me and saw all the DIVOTS.

DODGEBALL *(noun)*

a game in which asthmatic and obese children are rapidly pummeled with a large rubber ball; a very important schoolyard activity that teaches kids the value of being genetically gifted.

I was so good at DODGEBALL that my elementary school had to hire a second nurse.

DOUBLE DRIBBLE *(noun)*

a basketball foul called when a player dribbles with both hands; it doesn't give the dribbler an advantage, but it just looks too silly not to be a foul.

Man, just because we're playing a pickup game doesn't mean you can DOUBLE DRIBBLE.

DUDE, DON'T SAY IT: DINNER THEATER

What It Means: the only thing more annoying than a normal food server is one who forgets to refill your iced tea because he's too busy trying to convince you it was the busboy who killed the hostess. **It's Only Okay When:** a sudden urge strikes to combine shitty acting with mediocre prime rib.

DRAGSTER *(noun)*

the only time a man can say "That is one hot dragster" is when referring to the specific type of automobile used for drag racing; also means the man who drives the drag-racing automobile.

When told my dad I wanted to be a DRAGSTER when I grew up, he got a worried look on his face, then took me to a strip club.

DRIFTING *(verb)*

a pretty hardcore drag-race technique characterized by skidding out, or "drifting," through the turns. A very important word to know if you're ever trying to figure out which *Fast and Furious* movie not to rent.

DRIFTING is pretty badass—but you want to get out of the way if the car starts to drift in your direction.

ESPN *(noun)*
a cable sports channel that plays a crucial role in helping men ignore their wives and girlfriends.
> She was like, "I'm pregnant," and I was like, "Can we talk about that later, I'm watching ESPN."

> *I'm fortunate. The NFL Network is on Channel 25, ESPN is Channel 26 and ESPN2 is Channel 27, . . . I get the trifecta right there.*
> MARK CAMPBELL

ESPN2 *(noun)*
the most important TV channel for keeping a man up to speed on the latest jai alai scores, Ping-Pong star sex orgies, and which professional bowlers just got tracheotomies.
> Last time I went to a sports bar, I nearly got my ass kicked when I asked the bartender to turn off basketball, and turn on ESPN2 so I could watch billiards.

EXTREME SPORTS *(noun)*
any sport that involves high risk and amazing tricks.
> The suburban kid said he loves competing in EXTREME SPORTS because it allows him to experience an out-of-this-world adrenaline rush.

FANTASY FOOTBALL LEAGUE *(noun)*
a group of men playing make-believe, but with the use of athletic statistics.
> That guy who was arrested for running naked through the mall is in my FANTASY FOOTBALL LEAGUE.

FIRING RANGE (noun)

a place men go to shoot their handguns. Larger shotguns are reserved for outdoor shooting, such as when hunting friends of vice presidents.

A trip to the FIRING RANGE feels just as good as a trip to the massage parlor—and there's never a chance of the firing target being an undercover cop.

FLAG FOOTBALL (noun)

a cross between drill team and football; a favorite activity of women who want to play football, but aren't interested in taking a helmet to the uterus.

I used to play FLAG FOOTBALL, but then I realized it made me look like a girl.

FOOTBALL (noun)

in America, it's a name for a sport in which men slam into each other while trying to advance a ball into an end zone. Everywhere else in the world, it's the name of a widely popular form of interpretive dance.

When that Norwegian dude at work stops calling soccer FOOTBALL, I'll stop calling Norway Sweden.

FOUL (noun, verb)

means a violation of the rules; yelled frequently by former high school basketball stars competing in pickup games at their local YMCA.

Dude, you can't call FOUL every time that guy beats you to the rebound.

DUDE, DON'T SAY IT: FENG SHUI

What It Means: the art of arranging furniture in such a way that it would maximize a person's happiness if he were Chinese.

It's Only Okay When: explaining to a date why your dog's water bowl is in the shower.

MANWORDS

FREE KICK *(noun)*

in soccer, when a player is allowed to kick the ball free of defenders.

Soccer would actually be enjoyable to watch if, instead of FREE KICKS, they had free kicks in the balls.

FRUIT CUP *(noun)*

jockstrap.

When John forgot to wear his FRUIT CUP, his kiwis got a little bruised.

DUDE, DON'T SAY IT: FINGER SANDWICHES

What It Means: little, snack-sized sandwiches served at soirees and other lame functions. Why eat several little sandwiches when you can just eat a single giant one?

It's Only Okay When: you forgot to bring food to a party, and so instead just chop up an old hoagie.

GAME PLAN *(noun)*

a premeditated strategy to win a game; men are always advised to have a game plan no matter what they're doing.

The GAME PLAN at the casino buffet was to hit the roast beef section first, and then the unlimited crab legs, followed by the dessert bar.

GANGBUSTERS *(adjective)*

with great speed and force; best used to describe athletic prowess.

The golfer went GANGBUSTERS during the PGA Tour.

GONER *(noun)*
someone who has lost or is almost dead; best used to describe professional fighters, or rich teenagers who somehow think they're qualified to sail/fly/ bike around the world without parental supervision.

We thought the boxer was a GONER when he wouldn't open his eyes. Turns out they were just swollen shut.

GRAPE SMUGGLERS *(noun)*
Speedo.

Joe was shell-shocked by the large amount of old, overweight men wearing GRAPE SMUGGLERS on the cruise.

GROIN *(noun)*
the area in which the testicles live; best used for discussing sporting injuries without giggling.

I pulled my GROIN muscle, so Coach benched me for the week.

GROMMET *(noun)*
a young, inexperienced, but totally hyped skateboarder or surfer; if a man brings one to talk to girls, it's almost as effective as having a puppy.

That GROMMET doesn't even know it, but he was just my wingman.

GYM RAT *(noun)*
someone who spends a lot of time in a gym, either training for a particular event, or as a distraction from other life problems.

The filthy old boxing club was filled with GYM RATS.

HGH *[human growth hormone] (noun)*
an amazing synthetic hormone that makes a man feel younger, stronger, faster, and more virile, and eventually leads a man to develop the head and arms of a gorilla and the penis of an infant, after which he'll flee society to live in the forest.

We weren't sure if Paul was using HGH, but I bet his wife knew.

HIGH-FIVE (noun)

a type of handshake-like greeting in which one person will present his palm for another to slap with his or her palm.

A HIGH-FIVE is like a fist bump for baby boomers.

HOLE IN ONE (noun)

a very rare golf shot in which the ball's driven from the tee into the hole in a single shot; men more frequently use this term to describe anything that usually takes several steps, but was accomplished in one.

I walked up and asked, "Can I buy you a drink" and she said, "I'm not thirsty, let's just go back to your place." HOLE IN ONE!

HOME RUN (noun)

to score in baseball; to score in sex; to do something perfectly and completely.

The ideal HOME RUN: While playing coed softball, hitting the ball out of the park, copulating with all the hot female first, second, and third basewomen (and receiving fellatio from the big-breasted shortstop), and then, even though you don't have to slide home, doing so anyway to kick the catcher you hate in the nuts.

HOOLIGAN (noun)

a young guy who likes to fight, especially in the stands at games after the team they live through vicariously fails to score enough goals to give them any sense of self-worth.

Those HOOLIGANS thought they were something special . . . until the cops showed up.

JOCK (noun)

derogatory term for an athlete; best used to describe the bald, fat PE teacher who still tries to fit into his high school letterman's jacket.

The JOCK stuck me in my locker, but in his defense, I did accidentally make eye contact with his girlfriend.

JOCKEY *(noun)*
a midget who beats the shit out of a horse with a whip.
> The only thing that pisses more than a racehorse is a JOCKEY who took diuretics to lose some weight.

JOCKSTRAP *(noun)*
a hard plastic cup worn during sports to protect the nuts; a tribal headband high school seniors customarily bestow upon incoming freshmen during the first day of football tryouts.
> That one freshman looks like Groucho Marx with my JOCKSTRAP on his face.

> *Attitudes to museums have changed. If it had Marilyn Monroe's knickers or Laurence Olivier's JOCKSTRAP they would flock to it.*
> JONATHAN MILLER

JUKE *(verb)*
to move in such a way so as to deceive a defender, and cause him to miss.
> A pissed-on floor confirmed that the toilet bowl had JUKED the drunken football star.

JUMP THE SHARK *(phrase)*
the moment at which something becomes so ridiculous that it sucks, such as an end-zone dance that's been choreographed.
> Professional wrestling really JUMPED THE SHARK when Lawrence Taylor got in the ring.

LUXURY BOX *(noun)*
the first-class seats at a sporting event; they are suites that provide catering and secluded viewing of a game.
> The cameraman had to quickly pan away when he accidentally caught a shot of Paris Hilton's LUXURY BOX.

DUDE, DON'T SAY IT: LET IT COOL OFF

What It Means: to not eat your food piping hot off the grill. If men wanted to let something cool, then they'd eat something cold. Burnt taste buds are a small price to pay for not having to wait three minutes to eat.
It's Only Okay When: you just put beer in the ice chest.

MOTORCYCLE (*noun*)
something a man who loves the exhilaration of having a short lifespan drives.

There's nothing like the rush you get from having a revved up MOTORCYCLE between your legs.

MUFF [*to muff up*] (*verb, noun*)
to mess something up, such as a kickoff; also is slang for a woman's pubic hair.

She really MUFFED up her bikini wax.

DUDE, DON'T SAY IT: MAKEOVER

What It Means: the act of changing a woman's hair, clothes, and makeup so that people hardly recognize her, which is apparently something she wants.
It's Only Okay When: suggesting what a girlfriend should get so that she looks more like the women you imagine during sex.

MUSCLE CAR (*noun*)
a sports car with an engine big and loud enough to remove all doubt that the driver isn't the same pussy he was before he bought it.

I used to be afraid of the dark, but now that I own a MUSCLE CAR, I know that if something tries to get me, it'll turn itself on and bust through the house to protect me.

MUSCLEHEAD *(noun)*
a guy who lift weights so much, and is so into his physique, that he can't see how weird it is that he shaves his arms.

I want to become a MUSCLEHEAD just so I can wear lime-green tank-tops and shave my legs and not feel like a chick.

NOSEBLEED SECTION *(noun)*
seats in a sporting arena that are so high up, the thin atmosphere just might cause nosebleeds; best used when criticizing the terrible seats a friend purchased.

We tailgated for three hours before the game, so it didn't matter that we were in the NOSEBLEED SECTION.

 **NOT PLAYING WITH A FULL DECK** *(phrase)*
borrowed from poker lingo, it means to be stupid or not have all one's faculties.

It's advantageous to play poker against someone who is NOT PLAYING WITH A FULL DECK. Who knows what they're going to do!

DUDE, DON'T SAY IT: NOSEGAY

What It Means: a small bunch of flowers; consequently the only people who call flowers nosegays are involved in musical theater, and should thus be avoided—unless a man wishes to date the only type of woman crazier than a regular actress.
It's Only Okay When: sorry, it's never okay.

ONSIDE KICK *(noun)*
in football, when the team kicking off tries to have the ball go ten yards so they can attempt to recover it and maintain possession.

Recovering an ONSIDE KICK during a coed football game is how I met your mother.

OUTBOARD MOTOR *(noun)*
an engine that clamps onto the outside of a boat; when running it makes the same sound as when a man places his head between a nice set of breasts and blows into the skin.
> **Whenever I see the OUTBOARD MOTOR on my new bass troller, I miss my well-endowed ex-wife.**

OUT-OF-BOUNDS *(adjective, adverb)*
a ball that leaves the area of play. However, most guys will use the sports term to describe anything that shouldn't be done or talked about.
> **Peeing in the shower at the gym is OUT-OF-BOUNDS.**

PAINT BALL *(noun)*
a game in which grown men run around obstacle courses and shoot each other with paint bullets; it's just like a real war except reparations are paid by buying the winner drinks.
> **My girlfriend said she wanted to play PAINT BALL, but I knew she wouldn't enjoy any sport that might mess up her manicure.**

PHENOM *(noun)*
an unusually gifted athlete; best used during sentencing hearings.
> **If only the football PHENOM didn't also excel at breaking and entering.**

DUDE, DON'T SAY IT: PLATONIC RELATIONSHIP

What It Means: a girl who does not want to have sex with a guy, but still wants him to drive her to the mall.
It's Only Okay When: talking with your hot chick about taking your platonic relationship to the next level.

PIGSKIN (*noun*)
slang for a football.
> Brett and his son like to toss the PIGSKIN around in the backyard before the game.

PIT STAINS (*plural noun*)
underarm sweat stains in a shirt; every man should have at least three shirts permanently pit stained, just in case he needs to gross out women at the gym.
> My girlfriend was totally pissed about the PIT STAINS on the shirt I wore to her sister's wedding.

PIT STOP (*noun*)
a brief stop, usually to pick up some more beer at the liquor store, or to take a piss—typically in that order; comes from racecar lingo and therefore should be used as frequently as possible.
> We had to make a PIT STOP when we realized there were four of us, but only three pieces of beef jerky.

DUDE, DON'T SAY IT: ROMANCE NOVEL

What It Means: a collection of lies that give women false expectations of how men will actually treat them.
It's Only Okay When: buying a book for your wife at the airport bookstore that you're sure will be of greater interest to her than constantly asking what you're reading.

REBOUND (*verb, noun*)
to grab a basketball after another player's missed his shot; to do the same with a woman.
> Screw "bros before hos." My friend's ex was on the REBOUND and looking for someone to make her feel better about herself.

MANWORDS

ROID RAGE *(noun)*
when a guy on steroids becomes excessively violent.
> No one could tell if the female body builder was angry due to ROID RAGE, or the fact that she looked a dude.

ROOKIE *(noun)*
an athlete in his first year on a team, or anyone who is new to an endeavor.
> We forced the office ROOKIE to make a coffee run every day for his first year.

 ROPE A DOPE *(noun)*
a boxing tactic in which an opponent appears to be weak in order to lure the other guy into a trap.
> My girlfriend gave me the ROPE A DOPE when she said I could tell her anything and she won't get angry.

RUN OUT THE CLOCK *(phrase)*
in football, to strategically move slowly so as to leave the opposing team with less time to score; can also be used figuratively any time a guy has to stall.
> My wingman was running late and the friend of the girl I had my eye on wanted to leave the party, so I decided to RUN OUT THE CLOCK until he showed up to distract her.

DUDE, DON'T SAY IT: ROUGE

What It Means: a type of red makeup that women apply to their cheeks so as to seem healthy.
It's Only Okay When: letting a woman know that if she puts on any more rouge, she might as well go ahead and add a squirting flower to her lapel.

RUNNER-UP *(noun)*
the person who comes in second place; characterized by being a complete piece of shit, even if the difference between him and the first-place finisher was only a fraction of a point.
> The winner of the beauty pageant won $10,000, and the RUNNER-UP won a devastating blow to her ego and an eating disorder.

SCHOLARSHIP *(noun)*
a grant allowing a college athlete to attend school for free so as to fool him into thinking he's actually being compensated for helping the school earn millions.
> Despite having a full SCHOLARSHIP, Deion never attended a single class.

SHUTTLECOCK *(noun)*
the little white cone thing that people trying to play badminton will occasionally hit over the net; a word that's fun for guys to say.
> The drunk girl ran into the middle of the badminton game and became a total SHUTTLECOCK block.

SLAM DUNK *(noun, verb)*
in basketball, when a player jumps up and slams the ball through the hoop; more important usage is as a slang term for anything that's remarkably easy to obtain.
> Now that I've pimped out my resume, getting that new job should be a SLAM DUNK.

DUDE, DON'T SAY IT: SANITARY NAPKIN (AKA MAXI PAD)

What It Means: a diaper worn by menstruating women; the only time men should inquire about napkins is during a rib-eating contest.
It's Only Okay When: looking for something on your wife's side of the bathroom to help soak up some spilled motor oil.

MANWORDS

SLOT MACHINE (*noun*)
the least masculine of all forms of gambling, because if you lose, there isn't another guy immediately available who can be accused of cheating.
Every Sunday I have to drive my grandma to the casino to play the penny SLOT MACHINES.

DUDE, DON'T SAY IT: SILLY GOOSE

What It Means: a way-too-fluffy term to call someone a goofball; the proper male term is a "fucking idiot."
It's Only Okay When: talking to kids.

SMACKDOWN (*noun*)
taken from the very real sport of professional wrestling; means any confrontation or fight. It is the preferred word to describe arguments between wives and mothers-in-law.
When my girlfriend rubbed my knee under the table, it nearly set off a SMACKDOWN with my mom.

SQUASH (*noun*)
a game in which short, hairy guys with giant forearms run around a racquetball-sized court; it is customary for anyone who misses a shot to yell, "Geez, shit!" because it will echo throughout the entire gym and call attention to his failure.
I play SQUASH just because I look cool in goggles.

STATS (*plural noun*)
numerical data regarding how awesome an athlete is at throwing, catching, running, and scoring; collections of very important information for helping men live vicariously through their favorite athletes. Some men even compete against other men in leagues where they assemble entire teams of players they wish they were.
Even though the St. Louis Rams suck, I'm picking up their running back for my fantasy team because his STATS are great.

STUNT *(noun)*
in football, when defenders switch roles to evade blockers; in life, any attempt to bullshit or scam.
I don't know what kind of STUNT that guy thinks he's pulling by wearing a beret.

SUDDEN DEATH *(noun)*
a type of overtime play in which the first team to score wins; it is the only reason field-goal kickers are treated like human beings.
The player thought he was in heaven after his team won in SUDDEN DEATH.

DUDE, DON'T SAY IT: SLIPPERS

What It Means: men may wear sandals, thongs, or flip-flops. Slippers are worn by women and faerie princesses.
It's Only Okay When: telling your wife what's okay to wear to go out to dinner, just so she doesn't waste any more time trying on shoes.

TAILGATE *(verb)*
to party in the parking lot before a ball game; to drive with your car up another car's ass on the way to said ball game.
Some people think it's weird to TAILGATE at a child's soccer game, but the bars aren't open that early on a Sunday.

TAKE A KNEE *(phrase)*
when a quarterback intentionally stops a play by kneeling down, thereby running out the clock and denying the opponent a chance to score; this is done as a strategic tactic to make the end of the game suck.
My wife's favorite part of a football game is at the end when the quarterback TAKES A KNEE.

TAKE THE BALL AND RUN *(phrase)*

an expression meaning to take over a project or idea and develop it further; this is a natural activity for men who are always running with balls.

No one wanted to continue the project, but the office suck-up saw it as an opportunity to TAKE THE BALL AND RUN.

THE ROCK *(noun)*

slang term for a football; best used during a fumble because it rhymes with "drop."

Ever since that running back fumbled in the playoffs, he has not once dropped THE ROCK.

THE WAVE *(noun)*

when a group of guys raise and lower their hands, mimicking an ocean's wave, which is then mimicked by all the dweebs at the game until the JumboTron has done a complete inventory of every dweeb in attendance.

It is almost impossible to do THE WAVE without spilling your beer.

TIME OUT *(noun)*

the act of stopping play; also used by guys to either call attention to something, or stop some bad shit from happening.

Hold on, TIME OUT! You can't tell my friend you hooked up with his sister, and expect him not to want to kick your ass.

DUDE, DON'T SAY IT: TABLE RUNNER

What It Means: strips of cloth that are designed to distract people from how ugly the table actually is, and absorb any small spills.
It's Only Okay When: seeing how far the cat will slide when flung onto one.

TOP DOG *(noun)*

a person who is the alpha or leader.

I like to think of myself as the TOP DOG in my fantasy league.

TRAVELING *(adjective)*
a basketball violation in which the player holds the ball while illegally taking too many steps.

The center never gets called for TRAVELING, despite the fact that he's probably racked up enough frequent-flier miles to fly to Beijing.

DUDE, DON'T SAY IT: TAUPE

What It Means: this is a word used by people trying to invent a new color. Anything taupe is actually grayish-brown. And if you know it, it's usually because some interior decorator is trying to make something sound fancier than it actually is.
It's Only Okay When: you're trying to hook up with a cute chick who is into art.

TROPHY *(noun)*
anything that provides evidence of a victory. For hunting it can be antlers, and for material success it can be a beautiful woman who is young enough to be a guy's granddaughter.
I heard the X-games snowboarding TROPHY is just a huge, brass bong.

ULTIMATE FIGHTING *[mixed martial arts] (verb, noun)*
the act of getting in the ring and doing anything you can to kick the other guy's ass.

I would become an ULTIMATE FIGHTER if I wasn't such an ultimate pussy.

WAG *(noun)*
abbreviation for "Wives and Girlfriends," particularly those of professional athletes.

Since none of the WAGS were having their calls or texts returned, they naturally assumed all of their men were out buying roses for them.

WTF *(interjection)*
acronym for "what the fuck"; expression used to describe something really screwed up.

> When Adam backed my riding lawn mower into my pool I was like "WTF?"

> *Ever wonder why these words are flying? Maybe aliens in another galaxy will one day read this and think WTF?*
> FANBOYS

X-GAMES *(noun)*
a testosterone-fueled extreme sporting event, shown yearly on ESPN so that kids who don't like team sports still have an opportunity to watch Nike ads.

> My favorite thing about the X-GAMES is that it's one of the few times stoners and adrenaline junkies can agree on what's rad.

Chapter 7

WORDS TO KNOW JUST SO YOU DON'T SEEM LIKE A PUSS

(plus other words for sounding smart enough to get a job, get laid, or get a job that can get you laid)

Too often men are sidetracked by relationships and kids and work and forget that it's the little things that make life worth living. But fear not! What follows will help you forget about trivial details, such as your wedding anniversary, and help you remember what matters—such as anniversary edition *Star Wars* DVDs, Barcaloungers, and anything that makes you feel like you're twenty-one years old again.

A/C *(noun)*

short for air conditioning. But what is cool is that A/C is an abbreviation. Men should always abbreviate so they can spend as little time as possible talking.

My girlfriend wants me to fix her A/C, but I don't want to because when she's hot she walks around naked.

ACTION FIGURES *(noun)*

something boys play with to pretend they're other people, and adults play with to pretend they're boys. Note: Action figures are not dolls.

I was upset when my girlfriend told me my son was playing with dolls, but was instantly relieved when I saw him playing with a G.I. Joe ACTION FIGURE.

DUDE, DON'T SAY IT: BODY SPRAY

What It Means: perfume.
It's Only Okay When: it's your wife or girlfriend's fantasy to have you smell like a rose that screwed a piece of licorice.

ART *(noun)*

something a man says that he likes to appear sophisticated enough to bang a woman who wears glasses.

I think *Dogs Playing Poker* is my favorite work of ART, because I always laugh when I see them holding cards with their paws.

BABYDADDY *(noun)*

a dad, usually one who's out of the picture.
I tuned out when Marissa started to complain about her BABYDADDY's lack of child support.

BAIL *(verb)*
to leave; comes from "to bail out"; men are advised that only other men accept "I've gotta bail" as an acceptable goodbye. Chicks don't bail, they "catch up with you later."
> **My dad needs to borrow $500 to get my mom out of jail, so I've got to BAIL.**

BALL-BREAKER *(syn: ball-buster) (noun)*
someone who harasses or gives a hard time; some men are natural ball-breakers, and others must be rigorously trained through repeated hazing and mistreatment by older siblings, or a dad who's a real ball-breaker.
> **Much to my delight, my younger brother grew up to be a totally kick-ass BALL-BREAKER.**

BARCALOUNGER *(noun)*
a reclining chair specifically designed for men to get drunk and fall asleep in.
> **Once I turned fifty, I spent more time in my BARCALOUNGER than I did in my muscle car.**

BATHROOM KEY *(noun)*
a small key connected to either a gigantic coffee pot, plank of wood, or some other huge thing—it ensures that no man will steal the highly coveted key to the gas station bathroom.
> **I love this coffee shop, but the army boot they've attached to the BATHROOM KEY lets the entire world know I've got to take a dump.**

BATTERING RAM *(noun)*
an object for breaking through gates and doors. Despite being totally awesome, they are rarely used, because, at the exact moment a cop's about to smash open a door, someone inside opens it, and the officer holding the battering ram falls on his ass.
> **I practically had to use a BATTERING RAM to get to my seats at the game.**

BEEF *(noun)*
an issue or a grudge against someone.
> After he spent a few days with food poisoning, Greg had a real BEEF with the Chinese restaurant down the street.

 BELT BUCKLE *(noun)*
an ornamental pants-fastener that should be no smaller than six inches in diameter, and shiny enough to use for bass fishing.
> My blinging BELT BUCKLE doubles as a serving dish.

BOUNCE *(verb)*
to leave; comes from slang for a hydraulically bouncing a car as it drives away.
> I'm out of fabric softener, so I've got to BOUNCE.

BRAIN FART *(noun)*
accidentally saying something ignorant and stupid.
> I had a total BRAIN FART and couldn't remember the name of my date.

BRAINIAC *(noun)*
a smart person.
> The guy who invented the Jäger Bomb is a real BRAINIAC.

BULLSHIT *(noun, verb)*
just as the body is 70 percent water, so too is 70 percent of what a man says complete bullshit.
> She called BULLSHIT when I told her I was a Saudi prince—guess my four-leaf-clover tattoo gave it away.

BULLSHIT ARTIST *(noun)*
someone who is such a good liar that he's elevated the ability to bullshit to something transcendental and beautiful—like abstract art except everyone isn't afraid to admit it's bullshit.

> **I've wanted to work for a politician and become an apprentice BULLSHIT ARTIST.**

BURLESQUE *(adjective)*
a word one uses to hide the fact that he hired a stripper.

> **His fiancée agreed to our plans for the bachelor party when we told her we were going to a BURLESQUE show instead of a strip club.**

BUTT FLOSS *(noun)*
thong.

> **When she bent over I saw her BUTT FLOSS right underneath her tramp stamp.**

DUDE, DON'T SAY IT: BRIDALPLASTY

What It Means: when a woman gets so much plastic surgery before a wedding, that the end result is a face and breasts that could now probably do better than the guy she was planning on marrying.
It's Only Okay When: explaining to a woman what she doesn't need.

CARBURETOR *["carb" for short] (noun)*
mixes air with gas vapors to power older engines; valuable to know if a guy ever finds himself stuck in a conversation with someone who's into old cars. Not knowing what a carburetor is will be considered a sign of femininity comparable to wearing ballet shoes to any man older than fifty.

> **I don't understand why my AMC Pacer won't run. I even put a new CARBURETOR in it.**

CASTING COUCH *(noun)*
any piece of furniture on which someone with power takes advantage of those less fortunate.

    When I asked my intern to take a turn on my CASTING COUCH she thought I was going to give her a part in a film . . . it didn't quite work out that way, but at least she got something.

DUDE, DON'T SAY IT: CUDDLE

What It Means: an inherent flaw in the female genome that creates a desire to be held even after the sexual intercourse is complete.
It's Only Okay When: lying to her about what you'll do if she'll agree to first have sex.

CASTRATION ANXIETY *(noun)*
a feeling similar to the fear that someone will scratch his new car or mess up his new computer, except it's his nuts he's worried about.

    Johnny's CASTRATION ANXIETY kept him from being able to fully celebrate his girlfriend's promotion and subsequent pay raise.

CAVE MAN *(noun)*
anyone old and unrefined; characterized by not getting e-mail on their phone, and thinking the ripped-jean look is still in.

    At the museum, my kids got to see a real, live CAVE MAN, who was walking around wearing a "Frankie says, 'Relax!'" T-shirt.

I got my CAVEMAN club.
KOBE BRYANT

CHICK WITH A DICK *(noun)*
transvestite; pre-op male tranny.

    It wasn't until I got Maria back to my place that I realized she wasn't just athletic, she was a CHICK WITH A DICK.

CHIVALRY *(noun)*
a seldom-used concept in which a man shows courtesy toward women.
> I told the girl who had me do a tequila shot that I believe in CHIVALRY.

COMMIE *(noun)*
any pussy who recommends sharing something.
> I can't believe my COMMIE neighbor offered to mow my lawn!

COOKIE DUSTER *(noun)*
a mustache.
> Ned's COOKIE DUSTER made him look like either an old-time lawman or an asshole.

DUDE, DON'T SAY IT: CULOTTES

What It Means: baggy, saggy hippie shorts that are supposed to trick a guy into thinking she's wearing a skirt.
It's Only Okay When: explaining what your girlfriend should wear if she doesn't want to be the victim of up-skirt photography.

COP-OUT *(noun, verb)*
any lame excuse to get out of doing stuff; best used when criticizing a son or underling.
> My dad said I was using my broken leg as a COP-OUT for not wanting to try out for the football team.

COW TIPPING *(verb)*
to walk up to a sleeping cow and knock it on its ass.
> It's said that COW TIPPING is just a myth, but I don't believe it.

CRAPPER (*noun*)

the toilet; best used at a formal social event to let those at the guy's table know exactly what he'll be doing in the bathroom. That way they won't think he's leaving to be rude.

My wife shot me a dirty look when I announced that I had to use the CRAPPER in the middle of dinner.

DANDY (*noun*)

a guy obsessed with his appearance; oddly enough, this tends to hurt a guy's woman-getting ability, because no chick likes a dude who looks better than she does.

That DANDY actually does laundry and irons his shirts.

DEFILE (*verb*)

to make dirty or impure.

My three-year old DEFILED my car when he puked up Cheerios.

 DEMON (*noun*)

a pestering evil influence that has a way of screwing up portions of a man's life.

I don't get drunk to silence my DEMONS; I get drunk to party with them.

DUDE, DON'T SAY IT: DECOUPAGE

What It Means: the art of decorating stuff by covering it in other stuff; it's like writing a ransom note with magazine clippings, except that old people love to get them.

It's Only Okay When: explaining what you think the devil would make you spend your time doing if you were sent to hell.

DERIVATIVE *(noun, adjective)*
something a guy pretending to be rich should say he trades; it's actually a
financial instrument such as a futures contract, but all a woman will care
about is that it sounds cool enough to tell her friends.
> **I used to trade in DERIVATIVES 'till I realized they were all
> derived from bullshit.**

DIDDLY-SQUAT *(noun)*
something of which men have no understanding or knowledge; best used
when saying "shit" might give a grandfather a heart attack.
> **Playing *Farm Ville* all day doesn't mean you know DIDDLY-SQUAT
> about nature.**

DINERO *(noun)*
Mexican for money, because when people think money, they think Mexico;
best used to bribe your way out of Tijuana prison.
> **The con artist was furious when he found out that all that DINERO
> was counterfeit.**

DNA TEST *(noun)*
a test in which they see if you have the same genes as the town slut's fifth
baby.
> **I don't care if they do a DNA TEST. So many guys had sex with
> Rashanda that that kid ain't more than 10 percent mine.**

DOG *(noun)*
a really good friend, be it human or canine; best used as slang when homey,
bro, and dude have already been used that day.
> **What up, DOG? You wanna go to the park?**

DOG-AND-PONY SHOW *(noun)*
an elaborate sales presentation, such as an infomercial or political speech.
> **Despite the DOG-AND-PONY SHOW, he couldn't convince his
> girlfriend go to Canada with him.**

DON'T HATE THE PLAYER, HATE THE GAME *(phrase)*
what a man should say to blame his environment for his actions.

> **She's angry with me because I didn't call her after we hooked up. I was like DON'T HATE THE PLAYER, HATE THE GAME.**

DOUBLE-WIDE *(noun)*
as opposed to a single-wide trailer-park trailer, a double-wide has extra space, so that the enterprising meth head has additional room to cook drugs and copulate with relatives.

> **Wow man, your DOUBLE-WIDE is a lot more spacious than I thought it would be.**

DUDE *(noun)*
what one man calls another man when he's tired of calling him "man," "homey," or "bro."

> **That DUDE drinks a ton of grape soda.**

> *I hate the whole reluctant sex-symbol thing. It's such bull. You see these **DUDES** greased up, in their underwear, talking about how they don't want to be a sex symbol.*
>
> BEN AFFLECK

EARS LOWERED *(phrase)*
slang for getting one's hair cut; men should appreciate this description because it sounds more like a brutal surgical procedure than an act of grooming.

> **Love the fade, man. Did you just get your EARS LOWERED?**

EFFED UP *(phrase)*
a modification of "fucked up" that is suitable for kids' parties, or other situations in which people can't handle how *real* you are.

> **That call by the ref was totally EFFED UP.**

ELECTILE DYSFUNCTION *(noun)*

the inability to be aroused by any political candidates.

Bill really wanted to pull out that hanging chad, but when he got to the voting booth, he realized that he had ELECTILE DYSFUNC-TION and left without sealing the deal.

DUDE, DON'T SAY IT: EMPATHY

What It Means: knowing what someone else is feeling; to do so requires feelings to begin with, and therefore does not compute.
It's Only Okay When: explaining to children why they should feel bad for those less fortunate than they are.

ENGINE *(noun)*

something that converts energy to motion, and not just with respect to motor vehicles. The energy spent buying a girl drinks can also be converted into a certain type of motion. But a man should take care not to drink too much himself, or his engine could flood and stall.

You can tell a good neighborhood by the number of rebuilt ENGINES littering the driveways.

EXHAUST *(noun)*

the fumes expelled by combustion engines. If gasoline were burritos, exhaust would be its fart.

I'd drive a diesel if it weren't for the constant EXHAUST fumes.

FIST BUMP *(noun)*

rather than shake hands, two people will greet or congratulate each other by knocking fists.

I was surprised when the president gave the first lady a FIST BUMP. I didn't know that was official Oval Office protocol.

DUDE, DON'T SAY IT: FASHION POLICE

What It Means: people who believe that having a matching belt and shoes is somehow as good as actually being attractive.
It's Only Okay When: you're in San Francisco and describing to your wife what branch of law enforcement those men standing outside the bar dressed in uniform are.

FOUR ON THE FLOOR *(noun)*
a stick-shift manual transmission, with the added benefit of sounding like a doggie-style–type sexual position.
  I like my women the way I like my cars: with FOUR ON THE FLOOR.

GAS, GRASS, OR ASS! NO ONE RIDES FOR FREE *(phrase)*
an economic maxim stating that one may not have a ride in a guy's car without paying for gasoline, providing marijuana, or supplying sex.
  Women who see the "GAS, GRASS, OR ASS! No one rides for free" bumper sticker are always happy to know that the driver appreciates their sexual value enough to trade it for a trip to the store.

GAYLIGHTS *(noun)*
highlights in a guy's hair that make women think he plays for the other team.
  When Peter's fiancée made him get GAYLIGHTS before his wedding, we knew he was pussy-whipped.

GHETTO BLASTER *(noun)*
the precursor to the Walkman and the iPod; manliest of all stereos because they're unnecessarily big, heavy, and cause enough hearing loss so that a man won't have to pretend he didn't hear his wife asking him to turn that shit down.
I was late to the break-dancing competition because I forgot my GHETTO BLASTER.

MANWORDS

GINORMOUS (*adjective*)
cross between "gigantic" and "enormous;" best used to describe something cartoonishly large.
The tires on that truck were GINORMOUS.

DUDE, DON'T SAY IT: GIFT BASKET

What It Means: a basket, usually covered in cellophane, full of stuff like chocolates, wine, or dried salmon. But the contents don't matter. Men don't use baskets—they use buckets. When was the last time you went to hit a basket of golf balls?
It's Only Okay When: describing a basketball score in which the defender put up little resistance.

GOOD WITH HIS HANDS (*phrase*)
something said by women when discussing a guy who knows how to touch; also a polite way to say a guy's not good with his brain, or stupid.
He's no rocket scientist, but he is GOOD WITH HIS HANDS.

GRAFFITI (*noun*)
images and signatures painted by young men to mark their territory; it's like how a dog sprays, but with paint.
According to the local GRAFFITI artists, Veronica's a slut.

GREEN (*noun, adjective*)
a lifestyle where one wears ugly wool sweaters and geeky glasses, and has a miraculous ability to still get laid despite driving a golf cart.
I got sick of showering, so I decided to try my luck with someone who went GREEN.

GREENBACK (*noun*)
American money.
Tom was paid under the table, so his paycheck came to him in GREENBACKS.

GRODY *(adjective)*
super disgusting.

> I want to star on a TV show in which I travel the world eating GRODY food.

GRUNGY *(adjective)*
dirty, filthy; best used to describe a man's clothes, carpet, or preferred style of music.

> Susanne said that even though she liked John, his apartment was still too GRUNGY for her to even consider spending the night.

DUDE, DON'T SAY IT: GLEE CLUB

What It Means: a form of institutionalized sensitivity training through the use of show tunes.
It's Only Okay When: talking to a gay guy.

GUERRILLA TACTICS *(noun)*
unconventional methods used to achieve victory.

> The drunk girl resorted to GUERRILLA TACTICS when her boyfriend tried to keep her away from the tap.

HAIR PLUGS *(noun)*
hair that's been transplanted and imbedded into a guy's head so as to fill in any bald spots.

> I got HAIR PLUGS, because I hear women love it when a man's head looks like the scalp of a Barbie doll.

HAUL ASS *(verb)*
to move quickly.

> We'd better HAUL ASS if we're going to get to the liquor store before it closes.

HIGH ROLLER *(noun)*
a person who gambles for high stakes and takes big risks; like a rich poker player, or someone who eats at a Chinese lunch buffet at 2:30 in the afternoon.
The HIGH ROLLER was an expert at craps.

HIMBO *(noun)*
male bimbo.
When Jim couldn't figure out the tip, his date realized that he was worse than arm candy; he was a HIMBO.

> *He lusted after me, but I had to spurn his advances, because he's a **HIMBO**.*
> *I THINK I DO*

HOAGIE *(noun)*
a big-ass sandwich; no man should eat any sandwich that isn't capable of distending his belly.
I never eat a HOAGIE unless I also have time for a nap.

HOMEY *(noun)*
a friend from the same neighborhood; best used by white suburbanites.
Hey HOMEY, I heard you got promoted to regional vice president.

HORSEPOWER *(noun)*
a measurement of power based on the strength of a horse; one horsepower is equal to 746 watts, and is typically used for describing how quickly a car's engine can get the driver a speeding ticket.
My new car's got 400 HORSEPOWER, which more than makes up for the fact that I'm 40 percent body fat.

HORSE SHIT (*noun*)

something done very poorly; an untruth that comes from high up. Horse shit is a degree more untrue than plain old bullshit.

There is no way that's true. It's total HORSE SHIT!

IT IS WHAT IT IS (*phrase*)

the most important phrase a man can use for explaining something, since it essentially explains nothing; best used for excusing a horrible action.

Yes, I slept with your sister. I don't know what to tell you, IT IS WHAT IT IS. You said you love children; now you'll get to be an aunt.

DUDE, DON'T SAY IT: INNER CHILD

What It Means: a pop-psych term for the part of a man that's still pissed he didn't get a bicycle for his seventh birthday; it's impossible for a man to have an inner child since most guys refuse to grow up.

It's Only Okay When: explaining to a pregnant woman why having sex might be a bit weird.

IT'S ALL GOOD (*phrase*)

there are no problems, it's cool; best used when a guy needs to appear above any petty squabbles, even if in fact it's not *all good*.

I know I lost my job, but IT'S ALL GOOD. I'll get to collect unemployment.

JAWS OF LIFE (*plural noun*)

Jaws of Life pry open wrecked cars so that the people inside can be given breathalyzer tests and thrown in jail for DUI; a tool so cool it's almost worth causing an accident just to watch them in use.

Our car went off the road and flipped thirty times. They had to use the JAWS OF LIFE to extract us. It was badass!

JOE BLOW (*noun*)
the average nobody; men are advised that it's more respectable to be some Joe Blow (or Joe Shmoe) than a guy who thinks he's "king of the fucking world."

The man left the temp agency when his boss kept referring to general tasks as JOE BLOW jobs.

DUDE, DON'T SAY IT: JE NE SAIS QUOI (PRONOUNCED "ZHE NEH SAY KWA")

What It Means: a French phrase adopted into American art-speak; means "I don't know what." If used, people *won't know what* the fuck you're talking about.
It's Only Okay When: forced to compliment something that sucks.

KHAKI (*adjective*)
the color of pants all men prefer; suburban camouflage.
I made sure my new Hummer was KHAKI.

LEGIT (*adjective*)
short for "legitimate"; best used by guys who aren't.
Sammy says he's going to start working a LEGIT job, but I only give him a week 'till he's back in supermarkets stealing grapes.

 LIKE SHIT THROUGH A GOOSE (*phrase*)
the quickest something can happen.
I thought it was going to take forever to get to the party, but it was LIKE SHIT THROUGH A GOOSE.

MAC DADDY (*noun*)
a man with great power over women, like if Oprah were a pimp.
It's impossible to be a MAC DADDY if you work at McDonald's.

MAKE IT RAIN *(phrase)*
to throw money up in the air as one walks through a club to demonstrate to women that a guy is either rich or financially irresponsible; men are advised only to throw paper money, as a roll of quarters striking a woman on the head lacks the same aphrodisiacal qualities.
When my son saw a girl he liked at Chuck E. Cheese, he grabbed a fistful of raffle tickets so he could MAKE IT RAIN.

MANSCAPE *(verb)*
to shave a man's body hair.
I gained a few pounds over the holidays so I tried to MANSCAPE in some abs—my girlfriend was not fooled.

MBA *(noun)*
Married But Available.
There are a ton of MBAs at the bar where I attend Happy Hour in the financial district.

> ## DUDE, DON'T SAY IT: MANI-PEDI
> **What It Means:** short for "manicure-pedicure," a procedure by which women get their nails painted with the hope that it will distract a guy from the sasquatch-like hands and feet to which they're attached.
> **It's Only Okay When:** suggesting what your girlfriend can do while you're watching football.

MOOCH *(noun, verb)*
a guy who annoyingly borrows small stuff, and though he says he'll give/pay it back he never does; or the act of doing that.
If that guy MOOCHES any more cigarettes off me, I'm going to kick his ass.

MOON (*verb*)
to pull down one's pants and expose one's ass, usually while yelling, "Hey! Check me out!"; best done out the window of a moving vehicle at old ladies, who will be thoroughly offended.

> I was going to MOON the freshman cheerleading squad, but lost my nerve.

DUDE, DON'T SAY IT: METROSEXUAL

What It Means: a straight guy who dresses gay.
It's Only Okay When: a current girlfriend finds an ex-girlfriend's hair-care product still in your bathroom.

MULLET (*noun*)
a hairstyle worn by sophisticated men (and occasionally women) characterized by being long in the back, short in the front, and perfumed with cigarette smoke.

> When you buy a Camaro, it comes with a free MULLET.

NO BALLS NO GLORY (*phrase*)
an important male maxim stating that a man can't have cool stuff unless he is brave.

> Bob was nervous about asking for a promotion, so I told him "NO BALLS NO GLORY."

PARENTNOIA (*noun*)
the paranoia parents feel about their kids. Note: This is brought on solely by parenthood and not by the smoking of an illicit substance.

> Alexis's parents had such a strong case of PARENTNOIA that they followed her into the movie theater and sat two rows behind her and her boyfriend just to make sure they didn't make out.

PATERNITY SUIT *(noun)*
when a woman sues a man to prove he's the father of her child; if a man is ever facing a paternity suit, he should do the mature thing and flee the country.

> She slapped me with a PATERNITY SUIT, but there's no way that kid's mine.

PENIS ENVY *(noun)*
when a woman wishes she had a penis; can also mean anything women envy about men—such as the ability to pee standing up.

> Sandra finally got over her PENIS ENVY when she had her sex-change operation.

 **PIMP** *(out)* *(verb)*
to infuse something with a ton of bling.

> Susan had a fit when Bill refused to PIMP OUT her engagement ring.

PIMPMOBILE *(noun)*
a totally tricked-out ride.

> I hope my PIMPMOBILE passes its smog check.

PIT BULL *(noun)*
a totally awesome dog.

> My PIT BULL will kick your ass if you try to put him in roller skates.

PLAYED OUT *(adjective)*
not cool.

> I was so pissed when Jim told me that my skinny jeans were PLAYED OUT.

PLAYER *(noun)*
a guy who hooks up with more than one woman.
> Tom rethought his playboy ways when his (now ex-) girlfriend scratched "PLAYER" into his brand-new Caddy with her keys.

> *You don't play a PLAYER.*
> *FIREFLY*

POLYGAMY *(noun)*
having more than one wife; a practice common among Mormons and professional athletes.
> POLYGAMY may be illegal, but it's still pretty badass.

POSER *(noun)*
a guy who pretends to be something he's not; best used when questioning someone's credentials regarding how much they're into a certain type of music or sport.
> That guy's not a real cage fighter, he's just a POSER with a black eye.

POSSE *(noun)*
your friends; best used when in a gang fight or break-dancing competition.
> My POSSE looks very tough hanging out in front of 7-Eleven.

DUDE, DON'T SAY IT: PONY

What It Means: a cute, really small horse.
It's Only Okay When: describing a pony keg, which is smaller than a regular-size keg, and is ideal for weekday drinking.

PSYCH (verb)

to trick or fool someone by retracting a previous statement.

I'm pregnant. PSYCH!

RAINCOAT (noun)

a condom; men should always wear a raincoat, even if the woman says she has a built-in awning.

Just remember, a woman who can put a RAINCOAT on a man with her teeth has probably weathered many storms.

RICOCKULOUS (adjective)

so ridiculous that it blows "ridiculous" out of the water.

The fact that he didn't know how to use a compound miter saw is just RICOCKULOUS.

ROAD APPLES (noun)

dollops of horse shit that litter a road after a parade.

Brad was pissed when he stepped on a ROAD APPLE on the Fourth of July.

SHE-MALE (noun)

a guy who dresses like a woman, even to the point of getting or growing breasts with hormones; a wonderful blind date for a friend who owes you money.

I couldn't get over how many SHE-MALES I saw in Vegas.

SHIT A BRICK (phrase)

to be surprised.

The drug mule who saw the cops nearly SHIT A BRICK.

SHIT HAPPENS (interjection)

an expression that means "whatever happens, happens."

I don't know why your car broke down dude, SHIT HAPPENS.

SHITLOAD *(noun)*

a unit of measurement; generally used by men to mean "more than enough."

You want a free pen? Take ten! We've got SHITLOADS.

SHIT OR GET OFF THE POT *(phrase)*

a productivity mantra championed by overbearing fathers and controlling bosses.

Look man. If you're going to ask her out, then ask her out. SHIT OR GET OFF THE POT!

DUDE, DON'T SAY IT: SPANX

What It Means: a type of underwear that women wear to help create the illusion of slimness.

It's Only Okay When: telling a woman she looks so good it's as though she's wearing an undergarment that artificially improves her appearance.

SHOOT THE SHIT *(phrase)*

to make small talk.

George missed out on his promotion because he SHOOTS THE SHIT with the company's receptionist more than he works.

SOB *(noun)*

acronym for "Son-Of-a-Bitch."

That f'ing SOB broke into my house and stole my plasma! What an asshole!

SONIC BOOM *(noun)*

a sound made by a jet as it exceeds the speed of sound.

That was a SONIC BOOM, probably caused by an F-22; at least that's what it sounded like.

STAGE FRIGHT *(noun)*
the inability to pee in the proximity of other people, even if there's a big divider wall and there's no way anyone can see the man's dong; men should know that stage fright is completely natural.

I cure my STAGE FRIGHT by imagining everyone around me naked.

DUDE, DON'T SAY IT: STAYCATION

What It Means: when a man tricks his family into thinking that they'll have just as much fun creating a backyard fort as they would on a trip to Hawaii. Men should just admit that there's no vacation.
It's Only Okay When: threatening what your family will do instead of the trip to Florida if the kids don't put their shoes on this instant.

STD *[Sexually Transmitted Disease] (noun)*
What a slut gives a man in the way of a receipt.

I always use a condom to prevent getting an STD.

STREAK *(verb)*
to run butt-ass naked, often across college campuses or football fields; it is highly recommended that a guy be totally shitfaced prior to streaking so as to stave off hypothermia.

My crazy-ass brother just STREAKED the Civil War re-enactment.

SUGAR DADDY *(noun)*
an old rich guy who only dates young women.
Amber thought her SUGAR DADDY would put her in his will. She was shocked to learn that all she inherited was a pair of fuzzy handcuffs.

MANWORDS

DUDE, DON'T SAY IT: SWIFFER

What It Means: a type of broom-mop thing that makes most women happier than any man they've been with.
It's Only Okay When: buying your wife a Christmas present.

THAT GUY (*noun*)
who not to be.

> You see that moron hitting on a girl way out of his league? Don't be THAT GUY.

THE 411 (*noun*)
slang for "the information"; best used when a guy doesn't want to seem like he *needs* information.

> Hey man, give me THE 411 on that chick.

TIGHTWAD (*noun*)
stingy and cheap, primarily with money, but can also be used to describe miserliness in other areas.

> The college kid criticized his college girlfriend for being a real TIGHTWAD.

DUDE, DON'T SAY IT: TUTU

What It Means: a ballerina skirt.
It's Only Okay When: suggesting a Halloween costume to your girlfriend.

TIGHTY-WHITIES (*noun*)
tight, ball-hugging underwear briefs made popular by children, and adult men who wish to restrict their sperm count as a means of birth control.

> My doctor told me to lay off the TIGHTY-WHITIES if I ever wanted to have kids.

TMI

TMI *(noun)*

short for "Too Much Information." This is especially important when you need to make your friend stop telling you about what he did with your sister.

TMI, bro! TMI!

TRAILER PARK *(noun)*

a white ghetto.

If it weren't for TRAILER PARKS, *Cops* would just be an hour of watching guys eat doughnuts.

TWO-BY-FOUR *(noun)*

the correct size of a piece of wood for threatening to beat another man over the head with.

If that guy doesn't give me back my iPod I'm going to smash a TWO-BY-FOUR over his head.

URINAL CAKE *(noun)*

a scented disc placed in urinals so they don't smell like piss.

I wish every toilet came with a URINAL CAKE.

DUDE, DON'T SAY IT: UNDERWIRE

What It Means: a retaining wall for breasts.
It's Only Okay When: explaining to an older woman how she can prevent erosion.

URINE TROUGH *(noun)*

a long tub for group peeing sessions, typically used at sporting events or rock concerts.

It took me three minutes to get over my stage fright at the URINE TROUGH.

VASECTOMY *(noun)*
a surgical procedure that sterilizes a man.

I can't believe she made me wear a condom when I told her that I'd had a VASECTOMY.

VULGAR *(adjective)*
what a woman would think about all men if she heard them speaking to each other with no women present; crude and disgusting.

How dare she call me VULGAR when she's the one with the dirty mouth!

WIFE BEATERS *(noun)*
a type of T-shirt on which there are no sleeves, allowing a man a freer range of motion to swing his arms like a jive turkey when walking.

Nothing says trailer trash like a WIFE BEATER.

YUPPIE *(noun)*
acronym for "Young, Urban Professional."

Dude, you are turning into the quintessential tennis-playing, BMW-driving, sweater-wearing YUPPIE.

> *YUPPIES don't have loyalty. They have useful relationships and meaningful encounters.*
> WILLIAM KRISTOL

Chapter 8

BALLS, BONERS, AND BOWEL MOVEMENTS

**(plus other body parts and bodily functions
grosser than your grandma's goiter)**

There are times when you can get away with using
expressions like "trouser snake" and "crack one off" and
there are times when you may have to tone it down a bit
and use more polite language like "boner" and "balls."
The key is knowing the difference. Read on to learn the
finer points of mentioning the unmentionable.

BALD-HEADED CHAMP *(noun)*
penis; best used by those who see their penises as athletes.
> My BALD-HEADED CHAMP is never afraid to take a lickin'.

BALL-PEEN HAMMER *(noun)*
any word with "ball" and almost "penis" in its name must
be part of a man's vocabulary. It describes a hammer with a
round end commonly used in metalwork, but is obviously a
more suitable term for a penis that for whatever reason has
a disproportionately large head.
> That male porn star looked like a BALL-PEEN HAM-
> MER. I wonder if he's had collagen injections.

DUDE, DON'T SAY IT: BISQUE

What It Means: A smooth, creamy soup usually made from lobsters
or other shellfish. Any word with two silent letters is far too fancy
for any self-respecting dude.
It's Only Okay When: having to clarify to a waiter or waitress that
you'd like a bowl of that stuff that's like chowder, but more expensive because they won't serve it with crackers.

BINGO WINGS *(noun)*
the flabby upper arms typically found on schoolteachers and the elderly.
> Why is it that people with BINGO WINGS tend to have an over-
> whelming desire to wear tank tops?

BOLOGNA PONY *(ba-loney pony) (noun)*
the ideal term for "penis" when a man is with a poor woman who dreams of
being an Olympic equestrian.
> My ex used to tell me that my BOLOGNA PONY won best in show.

BONER *(noun)*
slang for an erection.
> Nothing starts a guy's day off right like a BONER.

BOOGER *(noun)*
what congregates in your nose when you have a cold. Note: Any woman with a booger should probably be avoided, as it's a sign that she might also fart, poop, or have other natural bodily functions.
> Nothing is more disgusting than watching little kids eat their BOOGERS.

DUDE, DON'T SAY IT: BED SKIRT

What It Means: a sheet that covers the space from the bed to the floor; any man who can identify a bed skirt is probably wearing a skirt.
It's Only Okay When: telling your wife about your favorite part of your room at the bed-and-breakfast.

BREAK WIND *(verb)*
to fart; best used when sailing.
> You can always tell when my wife BREAKS WIND, because she asks the kids if they need to use the potty.

*Being married means I can **BREAK WIND** and eat ice cream in bed.*
BRAD PITT

CANDY APPLES *(noun)*
an awesome ass.
> I wouldn't mind bobbing for Kimberly's CANDY APPLES.

CHILI CON CARNE *(noun)*
normally foods with multiple ingredients aren't dude food, but when those ingredients are meat, hot sauce, and fart pellets, it's a different story.
The carnival worker was very politically correct, and therefore would never eat CHILI CON CARNE.

CHOKE THE CHICKEN *(phrase)*
to masturbate; best used sparingly, and always when describing someone else.
I went into the back alley to take a piss and this guy was out there CHOKING THE CHICKEN.

CHORIZO *(noun)*
a Spanish pork sausage, or a guy's sausage, depending on the situation at hand.
My half-Italian, half-Mexican wife likes my CHORIZO with a side of meatballs.

CHUBBY *(noun)*
an erection; a term you should never use while banging a fat chick.
Pete had the kind of CHUBBY that a trip to a Weight Watchers meeting couldn't cure.

CIRCUMCISE *(verb)*
to have the penis foreskin cut off; comes from an ancient Jewish practice in which the foreskin is sacrificed to God—who apparently is really into that sort of thing.
CIRCUMCISING a horse requires a chainsaw.

COCK *(noun)*
a penis; best used when petitioning a woman for fellatio, or trying to bang a woman in the poultry industry.
After what happened last weekend, I had to have a doctor take a look at my COCK.

COIN PURSE *(noun)*
the nut sack; best used when a hot woman asks you to make change.
> I asked my wife to hold my COIN PURSE while I went into the dressing room.

COJONES *(noun)*
Spanish term for testicles.
> You have to have a huge set of COJONES to wear that banana hammock out in public.

CRABS *(plural noun)*
pubic lice.
> I didn't know my Sex on the Beach came with a side of CRABS.

CRACK ONE OFF *(phrase)*
to take a dump; specifically one in which the tubes of feces are so long that the sphincter must break them into bowl-sized pieces.
> I don't mean to interrupt, but if you'll excuse me, I have to go CRACK ONE OFF.

DUDE, DON'T SAY IT: CHEMISTRY

What It Means: what a guy and a girl have if they seem to be attracted to one another; the proper term for men is that "she's hot."
It's Only Okay When: making methamphetamine for your cousin's birthday party.

CURLY FRIES *(noun)*
a technologically advanced French fry in which the potato is curled, and enough sodium is added to dry a lakebed.
> I told the drive-thru person I wanted CURLY FRIES, but I got two apple pies instead.

DING-DONG (noun)
means both "stupid" and "penis."
That DING-DONG tried to put my iPod in my computer's disk drive.

DINGLEBERRY (noun)
dried balls of feces that have been left behind to dangle off one's ass; a common cause of skid marks. Dingleberries are more common in Type-A personality men, because they're often too busy to waste time thoroughly wiping their asses.
Warren Buffett has his DINGLEBERRIES insured by Lloyd's of London.

DIPSTICK (noun)
a penis, especially one frequently used to check fluid levels.
According to my DIPSTICK, ma'am, you need a quickie lube.

DISEMBOWEL (verb)
to rip out someone or something's intestines.
Man, I practically DISEMBOWELED that black bean burrito.

DONG (noun)
best used if you want to mention your dick in front of a girl, but aren't ready to make it sound overtly sexual.
Ouch! My DONG snuck through my underwear and scraped itself on my zipper. I wish it were smaller.

DROP A DEUCE (phrase)
how to say "take a shit" while dining at a fancy French restaurant.
Excuse me garçon, can you point me to the water closet so that I might DROP A DEUCE?

DUMP *(noun, adjective)*
an appropriate description of most single guys' apartments, and beautifully terse way to describe defecating. Men should say "taking a dump" especially when they need to cancel out something that's potentially emasculating.
    I didn't leave the room because I always cry at the end of *Pretty Woman.* **I had to take a DUMP.**

DUDE, DON'T SAY IT: DUVET

What It Means: a down quilt that is so soft and comfortable that any man who sleeps in one will wake up curled in the fetal position. **It's Only Okay When:** explaining to other guy friends what you slept on as a child, and why it's not your fault that you're afraid to bungee jump.

DUTCH OVEN *(noun)*
what is created when you trap a brutal quantity of potent fart gas under a sheet, and then pull the sheet over your girlfriend's head until she knows what a good cook she is.
    My fiancée put a DUTCH OVEN on her wedding registry, so I got that for her myself.

 FARMER'S TAN *(noun)*
a tan that only colors the head, neck, and arms. A guy with a farmer's tan should tell a rich chick who he's trying to bang that he got it running a triathlon, just in case she doesn't want to bang a guy who digs ditches for a living.
    I got a freakin' FARMER'S TAN when my girlfriend made me go pick blueberries with her.

DUDE, DON'T SAY IT: FIGURINES

What It Means: little statues that grandmas fill their houses with to replace the kids and grandkids who have left and never call.
It's Only Okay When: playing with army men, and even then they're only to be referred to as "action figures."

FART *(noun)*
stands for "First Alert for Rectal Torpedo"; best used when trying to make an eight-year-old nephew laugh.
When she finally let out a FART in front of me I knew she was girlfriend material.

FREE-BALLIN' *(verb)*
to not wear underwear, especially while listening to Tom Petty.
I forgot to do laundry, so I spent all of yesterday FREE-BALLIN'.

FRONT BUTT *(noun)*
vertically creased rolls of fat that hang down over a man's penis area, giving the appearance of having a frontal ass; best used by elderly men to repel the advances of horny widows.
My grandfather told me that he can sunbathe naked, because his FRONT BUTT keeps the family jewels from getting burned.

DUDE, DON'T SAY IT: FLOWERS

What It Means: things that grow in the ground that are killed and given to a woman as an apology; watching a once-living thing die makes women feel better.
It's Only Okay When: explaining to a girlfriend what you thought you'd surprise her with, what her cat ate, and why you were looking for an old shoebox.

MANWORDS

G-SPOT *(noun)*
nickname for the mythical Gräfenberg Spot, a super-sensitive bunch of nerve endings located inside the front wall of the vagina; something most guys can't find.

I spent so much time looking for her G-SPOT that I had blue balls by the time things really got rolling.

*What's the difference between a golf ball and a **G-SPOT**? I'll spend twenty minutes looking for a golf ball!*

IN THE COMPANY OF MEN

GLAND *(noun)*
technically any organ that produces a secretion; but more specifically it's used to mean the penis, the conduit for the only secretion men actively try to produce.

I can't come in to work today, sir. I have swollen GLANDS.

GNARDS *(noun)*
balls; best used when discussing someone who has been kicked, or through an unfortunate bicycle accident wrenched said gnards.

Never play football without wearing a GNARD guard.

GONADS *(plural noun)*
another word for balls, although technically, both men and women have gonads.

That player sure had a big set of GONADS when he scheduled two dates in one night.

 GRUB *(verb)*
to eat; a great word for men because it sounds like "grubby," and no self-respecting guy should ever eat a meal without getting at least half of it smeared across his face.

In some countries, people love to GRUB on insects.

HAMBURGER *(noun)*
what Americans use to worship the cow.
I thought suggesting we serve HAMBURGERS at our wedding was a great idea.

HAPPY TRAIL *(noun)*
the hair that leads from a man's belly button to his penis; it is an evolutionary trait that helps women perform fellatio in the dark.
I think she was pretty impressed when she found the pot of gold at the end of my HAPPY TRAIL.

DUDE, DON'T SAY IT: HOMEMADE

What It Means: when someone doesn't care enough to buy you something that's been professionally assembled, they will slap it together themselves and call it "homemade."
It's Only Okay When: referring to moonshine.

HARD-ON *(noun)*
an erect penis; and thanks to modern medicines, there are very few hard-offs—just the occasional brown-out.
For some reason, Bill couldn't get a HARD-ON until the lights were out.

HERPES *(noun)*
just like a king who conquers a lot of territory will earn a crown, a man who conquers a lot of women gets his penis adorned with a ring of victory blisters.
When she said she knew how to make my penis two inches bigger, I didn't think it would be by giving me a HERPES outbreak.

INCHWORM (*noun*)
a really small dick.
> Jane thought she'd be making out with a stud, but what she found was an INCHWORM.

DUDE, DON'T SAY IT: IT'S A GOOD THING

What It Means: this is the mantra of Martha Stewart, leader of all things decorative and vaginal. The only things a man should borrow from Martha Stewart are her domineering attitude and stock tips.
It's Only Okay When: telling your fiancée why you shouldn't wait for your wedding night to seal the deal.

INNARDS (*noun*)
guts, organs, and other stuff inside a body; best used to tell friends about the weird shit a guy ate on his trip to Japan.
> Hotdogs both look like, and are made from, an animal's INNARDS.

JISM (*noun*)
semen; best used by rapper Snoop Dogg to say the name "Jim."
> Jenny's firsthand encounter with Jeff's JISM was the talk of gym class.

> *We are gonna launch arcing ropes of JISM all over this motherfucker! Peace!*
> ZACH AND MIRI MAKE A PORNO

JOHNSON *(noun)*
every once in a while a name is simply chosen to also mean "penis," and that name is "Johnson"; best used when not near anyone actually named Johnson, or he might wonder why you're talking about him like that.

The history teacher was thrown in jail for telling his underage student about the JOHNSON administration.

JUNK *(noun)*
a man's balls and penis.

Don't touch my JUNK, screamed the hoarder.

JUNK IN THE TRUNK *(noun)*
a nice juicy ass.

That girl at the club really had some JUNK IN THE TRUNK. I think I'll try to get her number.

> *Aha! A little **JUNK IN THE TRUNK**, it's a Finch slam dunk.*
> *JUST SHOOT ME*

KIDNEY STONE *(noun)*
men possess the amazing ability to make rocks inside their own bodies just by not drinking enough water, and letting particles in their urine combine and calcify; and guys actually give birth to these rocks through their penises, and at the time of birth many men are so happy that they can't stop screaming.

To keep myself from peeing all night, I grew some KIDNEY STONES.

LOVE MUSCLE *(noun)*
a penis that is emotionally in tune with its desires.

Do they have a yoga position for stretching the LOVE MUSCLE?

MADAM'S APPLE *(noun)*

an Adam's apple that, for some reason, appears on a woman.
Turns out she wasn't a chick with a dick, she just had a MADAM'S APPLE.

 MAGIC WAND *(noun)*
penis; best used when trying to make one's virginity disappear.
I tried to use my MAGIC WAND, but it wasn't working, so she pulled a white rabbit out of her top drawer.

MAIN VEIN *(noun)*
this term came into use mostly because it rhymes with "drain." It is the preferred term for referring to a penis that needs to pee.
I drank too much beer. Excuse me, I've got to drain the MAIN VEIN.

DUDE, DON'T SAY IT: LAVENDER

What It Means: bluish-gray.
It's Only Okay When: trying to describe the color of birdshit that landed on your jacket.

MAN BOOBS *(plural noun)*
some men simply can't stand the unfairness of only women having breasts, so either through getting fat or developing a hormonal imbalance manage to grow a set of their own.
Kevin's MAN BOOBS were sore, leading him to believe he was about to start his period.

MEAT WHISTLE *(noun)*
penis; women are advised to always have one handy in case of assault.
I walk into a bar, and it's like for some reason only the dogs can hear my MEAT WHISTLE.

MEMBER (noun)

a penis, especially one that belongs to a particular group.

I put on my Members Only jacket and hoped my MEMBER would have a good night.

DUDE, DON'T SAY IT: MINIATURES

What It Means: very small paintings; one of the few things whose smaller size actually makes it more annoying.

It's Only Okay When: explaining what that thing under your bed is that has a picture of the Mona Lisa with a hole in its mouth.

MOOBS (noun)

man boobs.

Dude, those aren't ripped pecs. Those are MOOBS!

NADS (noun)

short for gonads, or testicles; best used figuratively to compliment a man on his bravery.

What a set of NADS on that guy who wore a sweater-vest to a hockey game.

NUMBER EIGHT (noun)

when someone visits a man's house, and during the span of three hours, takes four number twos, or three number twos and two number ones.

I can't believe that guy dropped A NUMBER EIGHT at my Christmas party. You couldn't walk down the hallway for hours.

ONE-EYED MONSTER (noun)

a penis that is capable of frightening people, but is really just misunderstood.

Dr. Frankenstein's wife begged him to create a ONE-EYED MONSTER.

PACKAGE *(noun)*
a large penis.
>Lou was embarrassed by the express delivery of his PACKAGE.

PASS GAS *(verb)*
to fart; this is the most technical fart term and should be reserved for explaining why a doctor's office smells like a biker gang shit in a taco stand dumpster.
>I PASSED GAS in class . . . but at least I passed.

DUDE, DON'T SAY IT: OUTLET MALL

What It Means: a bunch of stores that pretend to be discount houses as a ruse to get a woman to spend more time looking at stuff a man will have to say doesn't make her look fat; the only place worse than a regular mall is an outlet mall.
It's Only Okay When: mentioning to the local Chamber of Commerce what you think they should zone for a strip club.

PEE-PEE *(noun)*
what a male may call his penis until he becomes sexually mature. After that, he's more concerned with its other functions.
>It was really weird when that girl called my cock a PEE-PEE before we hooked up.

PENIS ELBOW *(noun)*
like tennis elbow, it is inflammation caused by excessive masturbation; treatments include creating an online dating profile, or in extreme circumstances canceling Internet subscriptions.
>I might have to postpone my trip to the masturbation nationals, because of an inflammation in my PENIS ELBOW.

PETER *(noun)*
like a Johnson.
>I kept trying to explain that the Book of PETER is not a porno.

PIG OUT *(verb)*

to eat like a disgusting slob; characterized by not talking during a meal and bringing the head closer to the plate; best used during the holidays.

The goat wasn't allowed to PIG OUT on Styrofoam cups after the petting zoo went green.

DUDE, DON'T SAY IT: PORTMANTEAU

What It Means: a word or thing that is a combination or traits or characteristics, an example being "bromance" ("bro" and "romance").

It's Only Okay When: explaining the word "bromance" in a book for men.

PINCH A LOAF *(phrase)*

to take a dump. This term has decreased in popularity with the rise of low-carb diets.

My uncle makes great homemade bread, but every time I eat some I immediately have to PINCH A LOAF.

PISS LIKE A RACEHORSE *(phrase)*

when possible, men should describe bodily functions with comparisons to the animal kingdom. As such, when a guy has to take a super-big piss, he must conjure the image of a huge horse creating a mud puddle at the county fair, so that his friends will understand exactly how big of a piss he has to take.

I regretted drinking all that Red Bull before we got in the car. Now I have to PISS LIKE A RACEHORSE.

*But after all those scotches I had to **PISS LIKE A RACEHORSE.***

MRS. DOUBTFIRE

POCKET ROCKET (noun)

Since rockets are shaped like penises, and pockets are near penises, it's only natural a penis should be called a pocket rocket.

We were all devastated when my POCKET ROCKET misfired.

POOP (verb)

to shit.

During Thanksgiving my toddler POOPED on the couch.

PORNSTACHE (noun)

a creepy 'stache often found on actors appearing in adult films.

Dave in accounting recently started sporting a creepy PORNSTACHE. I feel uncomfortable every time I have to file my expense reports.

DUDE, DON'T SAY IT: POSY

What It Means: a flower or bunch of flowers.
It's Only Okay When: singing "Ring around the Rosy"; since it's a song about death, it balances the use of "posy."

PRAIRIE DOGGIN' (verb)

having to take a crap so bad that the turd actually starts to crown, sticking its head out of the butt much the way a prairie dog might pop out of its hole. Best used when on a road trip with your mother-in-law as a discreet request to pull off at the next rest stop.

Please pull off at the next rest area. I'm PRAIRIE DOGGIN'.

PRICK (noun)

a jerk; a penis; best used when the penis is behaving like a jerk.

No matter how much I explain that I'm happily married, that PRICK still thinks I should make out with the sexy waitress.

SANDWICH (*noun*)
a preferred food source for men due to its simplicity to make, and the common practice of stuffing it with enough meat to constipate a gorilla.

If you add bell peppers, it's no longer a SANDWICH. It's a salad between two pieces of bread.

SHART (*noun, verb*)
a half-shit, half-fart; occurs as a result of a man not realizing there's a ball in the cannon.

The first time I met her parents I let out a SHART at the dinner table. Her dad's liked me ever since. Her mom, not so much.

SHIT STAIN (*noun*)
just as you can distinguish between the male and female of certain species of wildlife by characteristic stripes, so too can you distinguish a man from a woman by the brown stripe of shit bisecting his underwear. But unlike a peacock, the more elaborate the display, the less likely he is to attract a female.

I don't know why my girlfriend freaks out. My mom never said anything about my SHIT STAINS.

DUDE, DON'T SAY IT: QUILT

What It Means: something women put on a bed so that they may appreciate their grandmothers' skills and talents, as they beg their husbands to mash their faces into them during passionate lovemaking.
It's Only Okay When: asking your wife if the reindeer-pattern one or the snowman is the best for covering the wet spot.

SHORT AND CURLIES (*noun*)
slang for pubic hair.

I call my wife Shirley Temple because of her SHORT AND CURLIES.

SKIDMARK *(noun)*

a poop streak in a guy's pants; men should cherish this word, as it's one of the few to use car terminology to describe poop.

Derek's wife refused to do his laundry when he complained that his SKIDMARKS weren't coming out in the wash.

> *Why dincha just piss off, Fischer? Ya dotty wee* **SKIDMARK!**
> RUSHMORE

SKIN FLUTE *(noun)*

a penis that enjoys being played solo.

My ex-girlfriend was a virtuoso at playing the SKIN FLUTE.

SPARE TIRE *(noun)*

slang for a fat stomach; men are advised to always carry a spare tire in case their nightstand breaks and they need a place to set their beer while smoking in bed.

My wife asked me if I wanted to go to the gym with her to get rid of my SPARE TIRE. I said no, you never know when you're gonna need it.

 SPERM *(noun)*

the holy, special fluid excreted from a man's penis which, when connected with a woman's egg, creates the miracle known as life.

I've been jarring my SPERM in case I get into a car accident.

SPERM CANNON *(noun)*

penis; best used when a guy must use his enormous penis to disperse rowdy protesters.

So I said to that fugly girl at the bar, "Sorry honey, it takes something special to get this SPERM CANNON fully loaded."

STICK PUSSY *(noun)*
one of the more egalitarian terms for "penis," as it can refer to the penis of a straight man, a gay man, the penis of a she-male, or the masculine partner of a lesbian relationship. No one knows the origin of "stick pussy," but it's widely believed to have been introduced by feminist attorney Gloria Steinem as a means to promote gender equality.

I see breasts, but there's a chance some STICK PUSSY could be hiding in those sweat pants.

STIFFY *(noun)*
an erect penis; best used if a man wants his engorged shlong to sound like the name of a fifties-style diner.

Hi, welcome to STIFFY'S, would like to hear about our hotdog specials?

DUDE, DON'T SAY IT: SALAD FORK

What It Means: a special fork just for salad used by people who don't realize that a fork is a fork; no man should ever distinguish between silverware, for fear that his friends will find out he actually helps with the dishes.
It's Only Okay When: someone is freakishly born with two penises, and would like a pet name for the smaller one.

TABASCO SAUCE *(noun)*
a required ingredient on virtually everything a man eats; since men don't cry at lame shit like romantic comedies, eating spicy condiments ensures proper functioning of the male tear ducts.

The date when horribly awry when Jeff told Sheila that he wouldn't eat anything unless it was covered in TABASCO SAUCE.

TAINT *(noun)*
the area between the testicles and anus, or vagina and anus.

The bimbo put her gum on my TAINT when she took a visit downstairs.

THIRD LEG (*noun*)
one of the more optimistic terms for "penis"; best used when you wish to impress a woman with the size of your imagination.
> You'd think that my THIRD LEG makes me better at running marathons, but it's actually distracting.

THUNDER MUG (*noun*)
a portable shitter, often used during long road trips or at night when one doesn't wish to use a conventional bathroom.
> I just drank a ton of vitamin-infused waters, so my THUNDER MUG also has some lightning.

TIGER STRIPES (*noun*)
stretch marks.
> I felt like I was on safari when I saw her TIGER STRIPES.

TOE JAM (*noun*)
a combination of dead skin, sock threads, and other shit that congeals in between a man's toes.
> The difference between TOE JAM and toe jelly is that that jelly has chunks of fruit in it.

TROUSER SNAKE (*noun*)
penis; best used when a woman asks if a guy has any pets.
> Women are always very impressed to learn that my TROUSER SNAKE is a constrictor.

> Jay: *So you like animals, huh?*
>
> Justice: *Sure.*
>
> Jay: *That's cool. Even snakes?*
>
> Justice: *Well, you can't exclude an animal just 'cause they're not cuddly. Of course I like snakes.*
>
> Jay: *How 'bout **TROUSER SNAKES**?*
>
> Justice: *Ooh, what's a **TROUSER SNAKE**?*
>
> JAY AND SILENT BOB STRIKE BACK

 **TROUT POUT** *(noun)*
lips that have been puffed out with collagen.
Megan wanted full and luscious lips, but her plastic surgeon gave her a TROUT POUT.

TUBE STEAK *(noun)*
technically means "hotdog"; like any long tubular piece of meat, it is also a common term for "penis."
We didn't have a lot of money before you were born, so instead of taking your mother out to a nice restaurant, we just stayed home and I gave her a TUBE STEAK.

TURD *(noun)*
a piece of shit; a guy who acts like a piece of shit; best used to describe a mischievous younger brother who thought it'd be funny to poke holes in his older brother's condoms.
I can't believe that TURD stuck around until after the pool party.

UNIT *(noun)*
a penis; a measurement of penis in which one unit equals exactly one penis.
When I asked Vicky if she had her own place, she said no, but my UNIT wasn't one she didn't want to rent.

DUDE, DON'T SAY IT: UNREQUITED LOVE

What It Means: when a guy likes a chick, but she doesn't like him back.
It's Only Okay When: explaining why most teenage boys suddenly want to take guitar lessons.

UPPER DECKER *(noun)*

defecation in the upper tank of a toilet; this will fill the bowl with shit when it's next flushed. Best done as a housewarming gift, or to express disapproval about an issue with the owner of the upper-decked toilet.

I can't believe that prick took an UPPER DECKER in my newly renovated master bathroom!

DUDE, DON'T SAY IT: TWEEZE

What It Means: to tweezer-remove eyebrow or other facial hair.
It's Only Okay When: recommending to your mom what she might want to do to her mole.

URINAL *(noun)*

the thing men pee standing up in front of; what to look for if a guy's really drunk and wants to make sure he didn't walk into the woman's restroom.

If I were rich, I'd have a URINAL installed in front of my couch.

DUDE, DON'T SAY IT: UTERUS

What It Means: the place where sperm ends up if the condom breaks; a woman's womb. If a man knows this word, he probably also has an ultrasound photo of a dot.
It's Only Okay When: explaining to a child where he lived before moving into your house.

VIAGRA *(noun)*
a pill that causes boners; guys should not feel any shame about using a medication to compensate for the fact that the one thing that defines them as a man no longer functions correctly.
Ever since I got a VIAGRA prescription, my wife's been spending a lot more time with her book club.

DUDE, DON'T SAY IT: VARIETAL

What It Means: used to pussify wine even further by referring to it by its specific grape; the only variety of wine a guy needs is "boxed."
It's Only Okay When: robbing a liquor store to ensure you steal the good stuff.

WANG *(noun)*
a penis. Since Wang is also a popular Chinese last name, it's a great term to use when talking about your penis online, as it won't be filtered.
This girl on Facebook asked me about my WANG. I thought she meant my dad's old Wang brand computer from the 1980s. When I replied, "My dad has a wang, but I don't," she defriended me. Weird.

WAZOO *(noun)*
the anus; best used when recommending someone shove an idea up his or hers.
I told him to take his crappy idea, and shove it up his WAZOO.

WELL HUNG *(phrase)*
to have an exceptionally large penis.
My girlfriend actually had a bit of penis envy when she saw how WELL HUNG I was.

WHISKEY DICK *(noun)*

the condition of being so intoxicated that you can't get an erection. This may seem as if the penis is betraying its owner, but very often, the woman that the inebriated man is about to bed is so unattractive that his penis is actually doing him a favor by not getting hard.

I was so drunk that I was about to do her, but thank God I had WHISKEY DICK.

DUDE, DON'T SAY IT: WOMEN'S SUFFRAGE MOVEMENT

What It Means: the pursuit of women's right to vote; the only movements men should concern themselves with are bowel.

It's Only Okay When: demonstrating your knowledge of equal rights will force a drunken hottie to show you her tits.

Chapter 9

THEY CAN GIGABYTE MY ASS!

(words guys need for talking tech, social networking, and texting)

Not all guy talk has to do with booze and sex. Sometimes we need to talk about the tools that help us earn money for booze, or the websites that help us contact women for sex. Behold the world of science and technology! There used to be a time when these words were the domain of dorkdom. But now dorkdom rules the world. Here's everything you need to get your geek on.

APP *(noun)*
short for "application"—small smartphone software programs that fool a guy into thinking he's being more productive.
I have an APP that tells me how much time I waste playing with my phone.

APPLE *(noun)*
a computer company whose computers are a must-have for any guy trying to appear creative, and who believe having iMovie actually brings them a step closer to being the next Quentin Tarantino.
My new APPLE laptop is so bitching that it does everything short of making me dinner.

BACKUP, BACK UP *(noun, verb)*
real men never back up their files. If files get corrupted, men simply accept it as survival of the fittest.
The only things I BACK UP are my viruses.

BANDWIDTH *(noun)*
used to describe how much data a network can carry, and similarly how much information a person can process, or how smart he is. And with sedentary tech geeks, bandwidth can also refer to their ever-growing waistlines.
I'd like to hire your brother, but I'm afraid he's got the BANDWIDTH of a 1990s dial-up connection

BELLS AND WHISTLES *(phrase)*
extra useless shit on a computer or electronic device that no guy should be without.
My cell phone has so many BELLS AND WHISTLES that it actually has a bell and a whistle.

BLAMESTORMING *(verb)*
group decision-making on who to blame for something that went horribly awry.

No one was sure who left their dirty dishes in the kitchenette, but the BLAMESTORMING continued until Marty showed up and washed them.

DUDE, DON'T SAY IT: BOUQUET

What It Means: a fancy word for a bunch of flowers.
It's Only Okay When: buying roses for a woman to apologize for doing something that was probably well worth having to buy roses and apologize.

BLINDING ME/YOU WITH SCIENCE *(phrase)*
to confuse the hell out of someone by overloading him with technical jargon.

Don't get that gearhead talking about the rebuilt engine of his Camaro, or he'll really BLIND YOU WITH SCIENCE.

BLOG *(noun, verb)*
like a diary, but cool because you can post pictures of sexy women, or cats climbing screen doors.

My fiancée started a BLOG devoted to our wedding. Now everyone can go online and follow the daily progress of my emasculation.

BLOW A FUSE *(phrase)*
how an electronic circuit loses its shit.

The electrician said that if the homeowner didn't shut up while he tried to rewire the house, he was going to BLOW A FUSE.

BRIEF SURVEY *(noun)*
a long-ass survey that technology companies either e-mail you, or ask you to answer via phone when you call in.

> Sorry I was late to the wedding. Dell asked me to complete a BRIEF SURVEY yesterday.

DUDE, DON'T SAY IT: DOWN LOW

What It Means: to conceal a male homosexual relationship, not that there's anything wrong with that.
It's Only Okay When: there's really no other way to describe the relationship between your two roommates.

BUFFER *(noun)*
a storage space for a video, music, or other things a guy might be downloading; best used as an excuse for why a guy sucks at online video games.

> I'm actually really good at *Halo Online*; it's just that my BUFFER'S not filling.

 CALL CENTER *(noun)*
unlike tech support, a call center will also try to sell a guy new shit or services to go with the broken shit he is calling about in the first place.

> Oh boy, I hope the lady at the CALL CENTER asks me if I'll stay on the phone and complete a brief survey.

> *Mike and I are tuned into doing this right. If a customer calls me, I'm going to be in their office within half an hour. You're not going to have that response when the owner is in Florida and the **CALL CENTER** happens to be in Santa Rosa.*
> GAETAN TAMO

CAMERA PHONE *(noun)*

most phones these days come equipped with a camera and video recorder, which must be kept handy at all times in case the *Girls Gone Wild* truck pulls up.

I have a few pictures on my CAMERA PHONE that could end the senator's career.

CELL TOWER *(noun)*

strategically placed antennae that may or may not cause cancer, but definitely cause your phone to kick ass at streaming video.

My cell phone provider says not to switch, because they're about to install another CELL TOWER in my area, but I think they're lying.

CHAT ROOM *(noun)*

an online meeting place in which several people can congregate and lie about their age and sex.

When Jeff finally met Sally from the CHAT ROOM in person, he learned what "athletic upper body" really meant.

CHINLESS WONDER *(noun)*

rich snobby guy.

When I rear-ended that Mercedes I knew I was going to have to deal with some CHINLESS WONDER and his insurance agency.

CLUSTER FUCK *(noun)*

complete disorganization.

Our work Christmas party turned into a total CLUSTER FUCK when Lucy forgot to arrange the carpool.

COMMENT STREAM *(noun)*

a series of comments following a blog post or online article; characterized by being far more racist and rude than any human would ever act in person.

There's always one asshole who tries to pee in the COMMENT STREAM by calling the writer a communist, socialist, or racist.

COOKIE *(noun)*
imagine if a creepy stalker were a computer program. Cookies are placed on a computer by websites that want to recognize or track the user. However, deleting them can cause a catastrophe on the level of blacking out from drinking.

After I deleted my COOKIES, all of my favorite websites acted like they didn't know me.

DUDE, DON'T SAY IT: EXFOLIATE

What It Means: when a woman scrapes or washes the dead skin from her face, because she thinks that's what guys will be looking at.
It's Only Okay When: trying to come up with a commercial application for leftover Agent Orange.

CRASH *(verb)*
when your computer drops dead; often caused by God as punishment for excessively masturbating to online porn.

My computer CRASHED just when I was about to download an app that would've turned my mouse arrow into a fist.

CRITICAL MASS *(noun)*
the minimum amount of people or resources needed to make something happen.

Once I get two other women to say yes, I'll have the CRITICAL MASS necessary for a threesome.

 CTRL-ALT-DELETE *(noun, verb)*
the combination of keys used to revive a frozen computer screen or a software program. When a computer takes a crap on its user, ctrl-alt-delete is the sweet grandma who ushers him into the shower.

I keep trying to get that girl to go out with me, but she freezes so hard when I walk up, that I might just have to CTRL-ALT-DELETE the whole effort.

CUTTING-EDGE *(adjective)*
the latest and greatest.

My GPS has a CUTTING-EDGE feature that will actually criticize your driving, alleviating the need to drive with your wife.

> It's my guess that those **CUTTING-EDGE** artists who attack tradition secretly believe tradition will survive to enshrine them as the wild and crazy geniuses who destroyed it.
> BRAD HOLLAND

CYBERSEX *(noun)*
when two people use a chat room or other online means to simulate sex; men should be advised that, while engineers are hard at work building a gender verification system, at the current time there is no way to know if the person on the other end is a chick or dude.

Women like a man who goes slow with CYBERSEX. That's why I used a dial-up connection.

DUDE, DON'T SAY IT: EXTENSIONS (HAIR)

What It Means: artificial locks of hair that are tied onto real hair.
It's Only Okay When: you're trying to be a gentleman and ask a woman if her hair is real so that you may safely pull on it during sex.

DATA GLOVE *(noun)*
a glove that interacts electronically with a computer or video game; the only thing a geek will ever put on his hand other than Vaseline.

I wish I could think of other uses for my DATA GLOVE.

DEFRIEND *(verb)*
to remove someone from a Facebook friends list; men are advised that defriending a girlfriend is an acceptable way to break up.
That chick who banged me last week just DEFRIENDED me, but I think that's because she just wants to hook up.

DELETE *(verb)*
to think you've permanently removed a file or program; men must be advised that anyone adequately dorky or sophisticated can retrieve almost anything you've deleted.
Despite DELETING my MySpace account, my wife still found out I was the drummer for a Poison cover band.

DIGITS *(noun)*
a word used by men when trying to sound cool giving or asking for a girl's phone number. Saying "digits" is better than saying "number," but not as cool as having a girl grab your phone and enter her number herself.
She gave me her DIGITS, but when I called it was the number for a Pizza Hut.

 DISH *(noun)*
short for "satellite dish"; every man should have a giant-ass dish either on his roof or completely filling up his side yard—even if he uses cable.
I only get Animal Planet when a bird shits on my DISH.

DONGLE *(noun)*
sounds too much like "dong" not to be included in the male vocabulary. What it actually is isn't that important (it's a portable software anti-theft device that you plug into computers via a USB, ADB, or parallel port). The word has tremendous value as a means of talking about your penis at work.
The kinda-cute cougar in accounting requested I install a DONGLE in her old machine.

DOWNLOAD *(verb)*
to transfer a file onto a computer from some other computer or device; best used when explaining to a wife what's hogging all of the bandwidth and preventing her from streaming her soap operas.

Honey, if the lights dim it's because I'm DOWNLOADING ten hours of porn.

DUNGEONS AND DRAGONS *(noun)*
a fantasy role-playing game that is set in an environment similar to the Middle Ages—because who wouldn't want to fantasize about indentured servitude and the bubonic plague?

I stopped playing *DUNGEONS AND DRAGONS* at roughly the same time that I got my braces off.

EARLY ADOPTER *(noun)*
someone who always buys the newest stuff, even if there's still some bugs or problems, and the price is still ridiculously high.

Angelina Jolie has always been an EARLY ADOPTER.

DUDE, DON'T SAY IT: EXTREME MAKEOVER

What It Means: can be an intensive beauty makeover, or it can also be a major house remodel; either way, the only thing extreme in a man's life should be sports, or new flavors of Mountain Dew.
It's Only Okay When: a stick of dynamite accidentally explodes in your kitchen.

E-MAIL *(verb, noun)*
a way of sending electronic letters to a person or groups of people, primarily used to forward dirty jokes or pictures of babies that have fallen asleep sitting up.

I check my E-MAIL every minute, just in case my mom needs to get in touch.

FACEBOOK *(noun)*
an online social network in which men can prowl for long-lost loves, and then politely back out once they see a picture indicating that an old flame has actually grown into a bonfire.

I changed my FACEBOOK status to "married," and now I can't keep the women away.

FIREWALL *(noun)*
a protective barrier between the stuff on a computer and the outside network; not having a firewall is like not wearing a condom—things might run slower, but in the end you're better off.

My cybersex partner doesn't like it when I use a FIREWALL.

DUDE, DON'T SAY IT: FABULOUS
What It Means: homosexually excellent.
It's Only Okay When: mocking your girlfriend's excitement for the upcoming *Sex and the City* marathon.

FIRMWARE *(noun)*
software that's built into an electronic device; best used by men to talk about wanting to have sex with a female coworker, but not have it land them in sensitivity training.

I'd like to show her my FIRMWARE upgrade, although if she talked to me I'd probably still freeze.

FORWARD *(e-mail) (verb)*
to send an e-mail on to someone else that you somehow think they care about reading.
I FORWARDED an e-mail describing our national debt to my economics professor in hopes he'll give me extra credit.

DUDE, DON'T SAY IT: FEELINGS

What It Means: improperly channeled anger.
It's Only Okay When: describing what the end of your penis has.

FREE TRIAL (*noun*)
how a software company tricks a guy into putting its shit on his computer, and then once he's forgotten, charging him for it.

I have this new phone app that helps me find FREE TRIALS, but I'm still using it as a FREE TRIAL.

GAMER (*noun*)
a guy who is so involved with video games that he hopes to one day marry a girl who reminds him of his sword-wielding, big-breasted avatar in Second life.

The latest *Grand Theft Auto* says its violence is so intense that GAMERS will experience post-traumatic stress disorder, or their money back.

GEEK (*noun*)
characterized by a guy who makes up for an astonishing lack of social grace with the ability to perform a highly valuable and technical job; it is an insult if used by nongeeks, but geeks are free to use this word.

That GEEK referred to having sex as "combining ones and zeros."

I'm basically a sexless GEEK. Look at me, I have pasty-white skin, I have acne scars and I'm five-foot-nothing. Does that sound like a real sexual dynamo to you?
MIKE MYERS

THEY CAN GIGABYTE MY ASS!

GIF *(noun)*
abbreviation for "graphic interchange format"; mostly used to post embedded little videos in websites.

People who have GIFS in their e-mail signatures are under the assumption that a sparkling Christmas tree is actually worth my hard-drive space.

DUDE, DON'T SAY IT: FLIT

What It Means: to move lightly, like a bird; often used to describe young maidens who are "flitting about." The closest men should come is tiptoeing.
It's Only Okay When: describing the orgasm of a supermodel.

GIGABYTE *(noun)*
computer storage capacity. One gigabyte is a million bytes. Like penis size, a man should strive to have as many gigabytes as possible.

I got an e-mail telling me that I can add 300 GIGABYTES to my hard drive. I had to reboot just thinking about it.

GLITCH *(noun)*
a brain fart in a computer or electronic device. Men are advised that no matter how catastrophic the software or hardware failure, it is always to be described as a "slight glitch."

After the hurricane, their electricity grid had a slight GLITCH.

GPS *(noun)*
Global Positioning System; a tool that helps drivers navigate streets and highways, so that they are free to focus on sending text messages.
My GPS says that my date's apartment should be right here, but all I see is a crack house . . . guess I should have upgraded the maps.

HACKER *(noun)*
a guy who cracks into secure computer networks; best used for a man to explain to a woman how he's managed to get an American Express Gold Card despite being unemployed.

The government realized they could stop most HACKERS if they simply banned the sale of Mountain Dew.

HARD DRIVE *(noun)*
the part of a computer that stores a user's information, so that when it crashes and fails he can flip out, believing that his life's work is gone forever; very important so that men know which part of their systems to slam to the ground in anger.

I'm thinking the plant that built my computer was as corrupt as my broken HARD DRIVE.

DUDE, DON'T SAY IT: FLORAL

What It Means: having to do with flowers; the only flowers men should have anything to do with are the flowers that men do.
It's Only Okay When: When trying to compliment the pattern on a woman's clothes by saying something other than, "I like the flowers and shit."

IT GOT LOST IN MY SPAM FOLDER *(phrase)*
what someone will tell a colleague or employee is the reason he didn't respond to an e-mail.

No, I really like your e-mail about breeding a race of overly intelligent cats, and I meant to get back to you but IT GOT LOST IN MY SPAM FOLDER.

JEDI *(noun)*
a very powerful wizard with the ability to control thoughts, move objects without touching them, and live well past the age of adulthood in his mother's basement.

> I first felt the calling to become a JEDI when I couldn't get a girl to go with me to the freshman dance.

LIKE *(verb)*
on Facebook, to profess support or connection with someone's post. Liking something doesn't require one to comment on it.

> I "LIKE" my sister-in-law's comment about how even though today is Tuesday, it still totally feels like Monday.

LINKEDIN *(noun)*
Facebook for dorks.

> That guy sends me so many LINKEDIN requests that I had to put him in my spam folder.

DUDE, DON'T SAY IT: FONDUE

What It Means: cheese dip mixed with wine used for dipping stupid little pieces of bread; no man should have a bucket of melted cheese unless he plans to make a plate of nachos big enough to cause angina.
It's Only Okay When: a woman says eating fondue makes her horny. It's okay to eat gay food if it will lead to banging a hot chick.

LITHIUM ION *(adjective)*
the industry standard battery for most electronic devices. They're particularly cool because they've been known to occasionally and unexpectedly explode.

> The school had to give me straight A's for the year because my laptop's LITHIUM ION battery exploded and burned down my dorm room.

LUDDITE *(noun)*
people who are fearful or hate technology or advancement; best used when a friend refuses to check out your new phone.

My friend who just bought his first MacBook says anyone who doesn't use a MacBook is a LUDDITE.

MATH *(noun)*
the study of things women aren't good at.

The only time I use MATH as an adult is when I'm ordering fast-food combo meals.

> *Instead of having "answers" on a MATH test, they should just call them "impressions," and if you got a different "impression," so what, can't we all be brothers?*
> JACK HANDEY

MICROPROCESSOR *(noun)*
a computer's brains.

My computer's MICROPROCESSOR is vulnerable to the "I Love You" virus because, like any nerd, it just wants to get laid.

 MOTHERBOARD *(noun)*
the main circuit board in a computer; like a real mom, she'll stop talking to you if she disapproves of the sites you visit.
I got my MOTHERBOARD an upgrade for Mother-board's Day.

DUDE, DON'T SAY IT: FULL FIGURED

What It Means: what clothing companies call fat women.
It's Only Okay When: trying to get your ass kicked by a full-figured woman.

MYSPACE *(noun)*
Facebook's older, ugly stepsister.
I haven't logged into MYSPACE since I started Tweeting.

NOISE CANCELING HEADPHONES *(noun)*
headphones that actually emit a signal that beats the shit out of annoying noisy signals, thereby providing a quiet, peaceful environment; best used by professional athletes as they're filmed walking into a locker room pre-game.
It's amazing how my baby stops crying the minute I put on my NOISE CANCELING HEADPHONES.

ON THE SAME WAVELENGTH *(phrase)*
to share similar attitudes or thoughts.
I thought the sexy woman was ON THE SAME WAVELENGTH as me, but it turns out she didn't think playing with *Star Wars* action figures counted as foreplay.

OPTICAL DRIVE *(noun)*
a fancy way to refer to a computer's CD/DVD player; best used to justify the purchase of a $1,500 laptop rather than replace a $200 component.
Sure, I could replace the OPTICAL DRIVE, but then the other components would be jealous—best to just get a new machine.

DUDE, DON'T SAY IT: HIGHLIGHTS (HAIR)

What It Means: Multicolored streaks of hair—for women (and some men) who wish they were as attractive as Alaskan Malamutes.
It's Only Okay When: talking about sports.

POKE *(verb)*
a Facebook feature that allows someone to meaninglessly flirt by sending an annoying notification; best used on someone a man would really like to poke.

I POKED her, but it was the twenty-eighth of the month so I figured her system was down.

DUDE, DON'T SAY IT: LONG-TERM RELATION

What It Means: what a man can find himself stuck in if he accidentally dates one girl exclusively for about a month; it's like quicksand, except it often comes with new towels.
It's Only Okay When: explaining to your date what it was she said she wanted that made you buy a penis extension.

POST *(verb, noun)*
to upload a piece of writing, like for a blog; or the specific article that's been uploaded; best used to make any dumbass with a PC feel like a journalist.

Look, I don't want to explain to you why I won't go to Lilith Fair. Just read my POST.

POWER STRIP *(noun)*
a device you plug into a power outlet, which then allows you to plug eight plugs into an outlet only rated for one. Used by guys who have tons of stuff to charge, and who think it's manly to have to reset the circuit breaker every two hours.

I had to plug a POWER STRIP into my power strip so that I could power my 1 terabyte hard drive that I bought just for my porn and video games.

PRIVACY CONTROLS *(noun)*
a collection of obscure settings meant to confuse a person into allowing the entire world to know he is currently shopping at Bert's Big and Tall while listening to Eminem.

I knew my PRIVACY CONTROLS were wide open when a long-lost high school friend messaged me to wish me well at my colonoscopy.

PROFILE *(noun)*
brief biography and description on a social networking website; it helps to have a complete profile so a person can interact with people who like to lie about the same things.

Saying that you're ninety-nine in an online PROFILE is really just saying that you're over forty.

QWERTY KEYBOARD *(noun)*
a full-keyed, computer-style keyboard. Usually the difference between a smart phone and a stupid phone is that the smart phone has a QWERTY keyboard.

The QWERTY KEYBOARD on my phone was obviously made for someone who has the hands of a toddler.

RAM *(noun)*
random access memory. It's like the short-term memory of your computer, except that your computer can't damage its RAM by smoking pot.

I upgraded my computer's RAM, and now I can simultaneously download porn as I upload photos to my Match.com profile.

REBOOT *(verb)*
to shut down and restart a computer; saying you have to reboot is a much manlier way of admitting that you had no smarter solution to the problem than turning it off.

Asking if you've REBOOTED your computer does not qualify as tech support.

REMOTE KEYLESS ENTRY *(phrase)*
just so men know, unlocking a door for a lady from thirty feet away is just as chivalrous as opening it by hand. Better even, because now she can wait in the car while the man finishes his conversations with his friends.

I paid more for my son's bicycle because the salesman said it had REMOTE KEYLESS ENTRY. Too bad I can't figure out how to use it.

DUDE, DON'T SAY IT: MOMMY BLOGGER

What It Means: a woman under the mistaken notion that people give a shit about her family enough to read about them.
It's Only Okay When: you just can't get enough stories about kids who won't eat their vegetables.

SECOND LIFE *(noun)*
whereas women merely fantasize, guys build elaborate online worlds in which their childhood dreams of being sword-wielding half warthogs, half porn stars can finally be realized.

It's okay if your real body's a fast-food landfill, so long as your *SECOND LIFE* avatar has low cholesterol.

SHORTWAVE RADIO *(noun)*
a radio frequency on which truckers and hermits report UFO sightings.

I used to totally be into SHORTWAVE RADIO before I realized there are places called "bars" where you could talk to people without the use of electricity.

SILVER SURFER *(noun)*
an old guy who is somehow Internet savvy.

The SILVER SURFER wisely uses an image of a cartoon character as his Facebook picture so as not to freak out his younger friends with his old-ass face.

SMARTPHONE *(noun)*
a cell phone with the ability to access the Internet and get e-mail; men are warned that these days anyone who refers to their phone as a smartphone sounds stupid.

My SMARTPHONE has a feature that allows me to talk to other people just by entering in a ten-digit number.

DUDE, DON'T SAY IT: MOMS' CLUBS

What It Means: a group of women who congregate to drink lattes and let their kids steal each other's toys.
It's Only Okay When: suggesting to your weird bodybuilder friend where he might go to buy some breast milk.

SPAM *(noun)*
unsolicited e-mails sent from caring foreigners whose only concerns are making sure American men can grow bigger dicks, stay hard longer, and make a quick million just by helping a woman in distress get her money out of the bank.

I got SPAM from a woman saying that she saw my online profile and wants to screw; funny thing is that my profile picture is of Chewbacca.

SPELL CHECK *(noun)*
a program that automatically corrects a writer's spelling, effectively un-teaching him how anything is spelled, which becomes remarkably obvious once he must write something that doesn't have spell check.

I wonder if Snoop Dogg's SPELL CHECK accepts the word "foshizle."

SPREADSHEET *(noun)*

a type of software that allows guys to plot and grid data to discover trends.

I used a SPREADSHEET to determine that, for every time I tell a woman that her computer isn't configured correctly, I lose 1.5 chances of having sex, based on the fact that she'll also tell her friends I'm a dweeb.

DUDE, DON'T SAY IT: MOUSSE

What It Means: fancy shit that both guys and girls put in their hair; typically applied while the hair is wet.
It's Only Okay When: suggesting what that stuff is on the T-shirt by your bed.

SPYWARE *(noun)*

software that installs itself on a computer and then watches what you're doing.

I think my ex-girlfriend created this SPYWARE program, because after I sent an e-mail to another girl, a message box popped up, reading, "You're going out with that skank? I knew you always liked her!"

STATUS UPDATE *(noun)*

to add a message to one's Facebook page, or change an item on the page's info tab; men are warned that failure to change their relationship status from "single" to "in a relationship" within fifteen minutes of starting a relationship can very often end the relationship.

People who read Becky's STATUS UPDATE kept coming up to me letting know that I was not "in a relationship." It was nice to know.

STREAMING (*verb*)

describes a continuous download of music or video to a computer or phone. Guys should always be streaming something, because maximizing the use of technology is like maximizing the use of a penis—although it similarly increases the chances of downloading a virus.

If you're ever STREAMING porn to your computer, be sure the buffer's full or it'll feel like a tease.

DUDE, DON'T SAY IT: MURPHY'S OIL SOAP

What It Means: it's unavoidable for men to know about some cleaning products, especially when sponsored by NASCAR drivers; but anything other than Tide is to be referred to as "cleaning shit."
It's Only Okay When: asking what can get toner ink out of dog fur.

TECH SUPPORT (*noun*)

a group of people that a man pays $300 to tell him to take the battery out of his computer, then put it back in and restart it.

I called TECH SUPPORT because I hate money and love sitting on hold.

TECHNOBABBLE (*noun*)

bullshitting by means of using way too many technical words.

You need to download the plug-in and then do a ctrl-alt-delete just to check the application's bytes consumption, and then you should be able to do a proxy search for TECHNOBABBLE.

TEXT MESSAGE (*noun*)

the primary method of communication between a man and an angry girlfriend; the ability to not have to talk is widely regarded as the single best feature of cell phones.

I tried calling her to explain, but all she did was TEXT MESSAGE me that she couldn't believe I would compliment her friend on her new blouse.

TEXTHOLE *(noun)*
someone who texts inappropriately.
> My boss was supposed to run that meeting, but that TEXTHOLE passed the buck to me and spent the whole time LOL'ing with his girlfriend.

DUDE, DON'T SAY IT: MY EX IS A BITCH

What It Means: dates are like job interviews. If you bash your former "employer," the woman you're dating may suddenly decide that you aren't right for the position.
It's Only Okay When: you're out with a girl, and your ex happens to show up and insults your current date. Then bashing her can actually score points.

THE GRID *(noun)*
the national system of distributing electricity and other utilities; men hate being tied to anything, especially something that assumes they aren't capable of generating their own energy.
> I'm leaving THE GRID as soon as I figure out an organic source for online dating.

THIRD-PARTY APPLICATIONS *(noun)*
small software programs built by a company other than the original equipment manufacturer; best used to explain why a computer or phone has suddenly started running shittily.
> My computer crashed and I have no idea why. All I did was download this THIRD-PARTY APPLICATION made in the Ukraine.

TRACKBALL *(noun)*
a plastic ball used for pointing a computer's cursor; using one is a rare situation in which it's not gay to rub a ball all day.
> I find using a TRACKBALL allows me to waste time online much more efficiently than using a mouse.

TRUSTAFARIAN *(noun)*
someone who gets to slack off while his parents—or his trust fund—pays his bills.
    Greg was a really cool guy when we were in college, but now he's just a lazy, poetry-writing TRUSTAFARIAN.

TWITTER *(noun)*
a microblogging tool made famous by people like Paris Hilton, Ashton Kutcher, and other celebrities who benefit from not being allowed to say more than a sentence at a time.
    I have three followers on TWITTER, and two of them are my parents.

DUDE, DON'T SAY IT: PRINCESS CUT (DIAMOND)

What It Means: a square-cut diamond or gemstone; knowing about princess-cut diamonds means that a guy has been taken diamond shopping. The proper way to get a diamond engagement ring is to walk into the jewelry store by yourself, look at the price tags, and say, "that one!"
It's Only Okay When: trying to impress your fiancée by making her think that you actually know about the thing you just bought her.

UNLOCK *(verb)*
to take a phone that's only supposed to work on, say, AT&T's network, and modify it so that it can work on Verizon, T-Mobile, or if you don't like to talk on the phone much, Sprint.
    I UNLOCKED my iPhone and switched carriers because I thought I was missing calls, but it just turns out that no one was calling me.

UNSUBSCRIBE *(verb)*
the futile attempt to remove oneself from a mailing list.
    Those assholes make it so hard to UNSUBSCRIBE that I've just decided to block the sender.

UPLOAD *(verb)*
to transfer pictures, videos, or files from a computer to the Internet; men are advised that uploading photos of your drunk boss wearing a dress is a great way to get some time off.

I UPLOADED a video of my grandma cursing out my grandpa, and now I don't have to go to next year's family reunion!

DUDE, DON'T SAY IT: SADDER BUT WISER

What It Means: the motto of losers; real men are "angrier, and going to get evener."
It's Only Okay When: pretending a woman broke your heart, to score sympathy sex.

URL *(noun)*
uniform resource locator; it's basically a fancy name for a web address. Men like it because it's an abbreviation, and it makes asking what something's web address is sound way more complex.

Do you know what Amazon.com's URL is? Yeah, dumbass. I do. It's *Amazon.com.*

VIRTUAL REALITY *(noun)*
a computer-generated simulation of real-life experiences; used to train fighter pilots, surgeons, and horny teenagers.

In my VIRTUAL REALITY, women *want* a guy with no money and no prospects.

VIRUS *(noun)*
software code that gets into a computer, and then replicates itself until the computer or system is damaged or destroyed.

I don't know how my system got a VIRUS. All my programs said they'd been tested.

DUDE, DON'T SAY IT: TABLECLOTH

What It Means: tablecloths are nothing but a trick to create more laundry; do everyone a favor and insist on eating bareback.
It's Only Okay When: your wife says to bring a bed sheet from the linen closet, and you find something that's close enough.

VOICE MAIL (*noun*)

a cell phone feature that allows a guy to not talk to his mom, but also forces him to leave awkward messages for girls he meets at parties who weren't drunk enough to give him the wrong number.

That girl I hooked up with last night sent me to VOICE MAIL. I knew I should've done more foreplay.

ACKNOWLEDGMENTS

First and foremost, huge thanks to my agent, David Fugate, for making this book happen; with very great thanks to Peter Archer at Adams Media, who had the Joseph-like vision, as well as Katie Corcoran Lytle and everyone else at Adams for keeping the manuscript on track, and without whom many of these definitions would not be as good as they are. It is an honor to help make this book one of the most important and influential works in all of Western literature!

I am truly and remarkably blessed to have the strong friendship of Lane Butler, the faith of Nicole Ghazal and Gina Cohen, and the tutelage of Chris Federico.

I would also like to thank my great friends Andrew Norelli, Tommy Savitt, and all of the comedians, bookers, TV and radio people, and venue owners with whom I've come to share my journey. There are too many of you to mention, but you know who you are, and all are greatly appreciated!

Above all, I need to thank my wonderful wife, Barbara, for her love and support through the long hours, and my wonderful twin boys, Ben and Seth, for being endless sources of sophomoric humor; I would also like to thank my mother-in-law for not being a typical mother-in-law, as well as my mom, dad, Lauren, Jon, Ryann, and the entire Greenberg crew. And to my readers and fans: thanks for continuing to have fun!

ABOUT THE AUTHOR

💪 💪

Jeremy Greenberg is an internationally headlining stand-up comedian, author, blogger, and joke writer. He has appeared on numerous national TV and radio shows, and has done five overseas tours to perform for our troops. Jeremy has also been a contributing joke writer for *Comics Unleashed with Byron Allen* and *The Complete Idiot's Guide to Jokes*. He's also the author of *Relative Discomfort: The Family Survival Guide*, *Sorry I Peed on You (And other heartwarming letters to Mommy)*, and *Sorry I Pooped in Your Shoe (And other steamy love letters from puppy and doggy)*. When Jeremy is not performing or writing, he is at home in San Diego demonstrating alphamale behavior to his twin, three-year-old sons—mostly by yelling, "Whatever!" and leaving the room every time his wife says that he's incorrectly loaded the dishwasher. Learn more at *www.manwords book.com*.

DAILY BENDER

Want Some More?

Hit up our humor blog, The Daily Bender, to get your fill of all things funny—be it subversive, odd, offbeat, or just plain mean. The Bender editors are there to get you through the day and on your way to happy hour. Whether we're linking to the latest video that made us laugh or calling out (or bullshit on) whatever's happening, we've got what you need for a good laugh.

If you like our book, you'll love our blog. (And if you hated it, "man up" and tell us why.) Visit The Daily Bender for a shot of humor that'll serve you until the bartender can.

Sign up for our newsletter at
www.adamsmedia.com/blog/humor
and download our Top Ten Maxims No Man Should Live Without.